W9-AAK-271

CULTURE SMART!

GHANA

Ian Utley

·K·U·P·E·R·A·R·D·

This book is available for special discounts for bulk purchases for sales promotions or premiums. Special editions, including personalized covers, excerpts of existing books, and corporate imprints, can be created in large quantities for special needs.

For more information in the USA write to Special Markets/Premium Sales, 1745 Broadway, MD 6–2, New York, NY 10019, or e-mail specialmarkets@randomhouse.com.

In the United Kingdom contact Kuperard publishers at the address below.

ISBN 978 1 85733 474 6
This book is also available as an e-book: eISBN 978 1 85733 604 7

British Library Cataloguing in Publication Data
A CIP catalogue entry for this book is available from the British Library

First published in Great Britain
by Kuperard, an imprint of Bravo Ltd
59 Hutton Grove, London N12 8DS
Tel: +44 (0) 20 8446 2440   Fax: +44 (0) 20 8446 2441
www.culturesmart.co.uk
Inquiries: sales@kuperard.co.uk

Distributed in the United States and Canada
by Random House Distribution Services
1745 Broadway, New York, NY 10019
Tel: +1 (212) 572-2844   Fax: +1 (212) 572-4961
Inquiries: csorders@randomhouse.com

Series Editor Geoffrey Chesler
Design Bobby Birchall

Printed in Malaysia

Cover image: Traditional Kente cloth of the Ashanti people.
© Alan Tobey/ iStockphoto.com

Photographs on pages 43, 79, 94 (bottom), 96, 101, 117, 123, and 131 by courtesy of the author.

Images on pages 13 © Erik Kristensen; 17, 58, 66, and 107 © Ghana National Commission on Culture; 19, 24, 108, 112 (bottom), 121, and 124 © ZSM; 20 and 35 © Ricardo Stuckert; 26, 98 (top), and 114 © aripeskoe2; 33 © George Appiah; 37 and 48 © Guido Sohne; 39 © Stig Nygaard; 47 © Joerg Scherbaum; 77 and 130 © Hugues; 111 © Ferdinand Reus; 112 (top) © cliff1066; 113 © hiyori13; 116 © Antiker; 127 and 145 © Elegant Machines

About the Author

IAN UTLEY is a British teacher who studied French and Linguistics at the University of Wales, Bangor, before gaining a BSc and teaching qualification at Bishop Grosseteste University College, Lincoln. He has been learning about Ghanaian culture and languages since 1998 when he worked as a teacher trainer with Voluntary Service Overseas. He has since carried out educational research projects across the country, taken the headship of a Ghanaian school, and published a book for learners of the Twi language. He has also appeared on Twi-language television and radio shows in Ghana and is a columnist for the Ghanaian newspaper *Weekend World*.

Ian now works as an advisor to the Ministry of Tourism and Diasporan Relations in Accra. He also organizes cultural, ecotourism, and language learning activities for foreigners, and can be contacted at learntwi@yahoo.com.

The Culture Smart! series is continuing to expand.
For further information and latest titles visit
www.culturesmart.co.uk

The publishers would like to thank **CultureSmart!**Consulting for its help in researching and developing the concept for this series.

CultureSmart!Consulting creates tailor-made seminars and consultancy programs to meet a wide range of corporate, public-sector, and Individual needs. Whether delivering courses on multicultural team building in the USA, preparing Chinese engineers for a posting in Europe, training call-center staff in India, or raising the awareness of police forces to the needs of diverse ethnic communities, it provides essential, practical, and powerful skills worldwide to an increasingly international workforce.

For details, visit www.culturesmartconsulting.com

CultureSmart!Consulting and **CultureSmart!** guides have both contributed to and featured regularly in the weekly travel program "Fast Track" on BBC World TV.

contents

contents

Map of Ghana

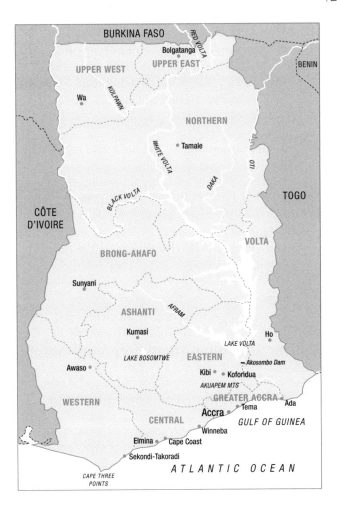

introduction

There is a tendency in the Western media to report only the negative aspects of Africa. The picture received is generally one of complete underdevelopment, primitive living conditions, famine, HIV/AIDS, war, and political mismanagement. Tellingly, Ghana is one of the African countries that receives very little, if any, media coverage.

Ghana, however, is a country with a rapidly growing reputation and currently welcomes around a million tourists, aid workers, and business travelers a year. These visitors invariably come away with glowing reports of "the Gateway to Africa": a country of scenic beauty, rich culture and traditions, and a plethora of tourist attractions. For visitors coming from developed countries with their associated problems of crime, antisocial behavior, family breakdown, disrespectful children, unfriendliness, loneliness, high cost of living, and terrible weather, Ghana comes as a wonderfully refreshing change, with valuable lessons to teach to the outside world.

It is primarily the people of Ghana who make the biggest impression. It is due to their incredible hospitality and love of peace that Ghana has a claim to be the safest and friendliest country in Africa. Ghanaians are very welcoming to foreign guests, respectful to each other, strong followers of tradition, and have deep familial and communal values.

A visit to Ghana is highly recommended for those looking for a different kind of vacation, and is a life-changing and eye-opening experience. It is not, however, without its downsides, and visitors do experience frustrations and barriers (which reading this book should help to disperse). Less impressive aspects include the roads, sanitation, timekeeping, and customer service. Ghanaians like to do things their own way, and Ghana is a proud country that does not cater exclusively to tourists but rather expects them to fit in with the Ghanaian pace and way of life.

Culture Smart! Ghana aims to enable visitors to appreciate Ghana, while at the same time showing respect for its inhabitants. Visitors are warmly welcomed, but Ghanaians will require these visitors to be sympathetic to their customs and beliefs, and will have no hesitation in saying, "We don't do that here," should a faux pas be made or a taboo broken. It is important to Ghanaians that they, and their guests, follow certain rules and codes of conduct. *Culture Smart! Ghana* will describe these rules, explain where they come from, and offer the reader an opportunity to get under the skin of Ghanaians and enjoy all that this beautiful country has to offer. Show respect and you will, without a doubt, be made to feel welcome.

Akwaaba!

Key Facts

Official Name	Republic of Ghana	Member of the Commonwealth, African Union, and Economic Community of West African States (ECOWAS)
Independence	March 6, 1957	Formerly Gold Coast, a British colony
Capital City	Accra (rhymes with "a car")	Population approx. 2.5 million
Main Cities	Kumasi, Tamale, Sekondi-Takoradi, Tema	
Area	92,100 sq. miles (238,540 sq. km)	
Geography	Sub-Saharan West Africa. Bordered by Togo, Burkina Faso, Côte d'Ivoire, Gulf of Guinea	10 regions: Greater Accra, Ashanti, Volta, Brong-Ahafo, Eastern, Western, Central, Northern, Upper East, Upper West
Terrain	South to north: coastal plains, rain forest, savanna; mountains in east up to 2,952 feet (900 m)	Lake Volta is two-thirds the length of the country.
Climate	Tropical; rainy summers, dry winters	
Population	22 million (2007 estimate)	
Ethnic Makeup	Black African 99%, other (mainly Lebanese) 1%	

Age Structure	0–14 years 41% 15–64 years 55% 65+ years 4%	
Natural Resources	Gold, diamonds, bauxite, manganese, timber, cocoa, oil, hydroelectricity	
Currency	Ghana cedi (Gh C) (pronounced "seedy")	1 Gh C = 100 Ghana Pesewas (Gh P); 1 Gh C = approx. US $1
Language	The national language is English.	There are 50+ local langs., incl. Twi, Fante, Ewe, Ga, Hausa, Dagbani, Nzema.
Religion	Mostly Christian; 15% Muslim	The remainder hold traditional, or animist, beliefs.
Government	Republic with tricameral legislature. Constitutional democracy	President is head of state, elected for four-year term. Longest history of democratic elections in Africa
Media	TV: GTV (Engl. and Ghanaian langs.); TV3 and Metro TV (English). Radio: Joy FM, Radio Gold, Atlantis FM (Engl.); Peace FM (Twi)	Newspapers: *Daily Graphic, Ghanaian Chronicle, Ghanaian Times* (all English); *Graphic Asempa* (Twi)
Electricity	220 volts (50 Hz)	Two- and three-pronged plugs used
TV/Video	PAL system	
Internet Domain	.gh	
Telephone	Country code 233	
Time Zone	GMT	

chapter one

LAND & PEOPLE

GEOGRAPHY

"Welcome to Ghana—the Center of the World!" is a message you're bound to hear or see from the proud people of this wonderful country at some stage during your visit. Although some very patriotic sign writers have been known to "stretch" the map of Ghana down a bit to support this claim, the actual "center of the world" referred to is some 200 miles (320 km) south of the port city of Tema, in the waters of the Gulf of Guinea. Ghana can, however, rightfully boast to be the closest landmass to the artificial "center" created by the intersection of the Equator and the Greenwich Meridian.

Ghana can be referred to as being under the "armpit" of Africa, in the middle of the West African sub-Saharan region. (West Africa: Best Africa.) The "trigger" of Africa is another term used, imagining that Africa could be held as a gun. This term also alludes to Ghana's reputation as a respected and influential nation on the continent. Ghana is surrounded by French-speaking countries: Côte d'Ivoire to the west, Burkina Faso, then Mali and Niger to the north, and Togo, then Benin to the east. (Despite these neighbors, hardly any Ghanaians speak French.)

The waters of the Gulf of Guinea on the south coast become the Atlantic Ocean.

The landscape of Ghana is predominantly formed by the ancient Precambrian shield, rich in mineral resources. The country has a total area of 92,100 sq. miles (238,540 sq. km), similar to the size of Britain or the US state of Oregon, and is roughly rectangular, around 419 miles (670 km) north to south and 312 miles (500 km) east to west. It lies between latitudes 4 and 11 degrees north and 3 and 1 degrees east. The southern border is slightly longer than the northern border, with around 344 miles (550 km) of beautiful coastline to explore.

This rectangle passes through several vegetation zones differentiated mainly by their rainfall. Southerly winds bring moisture-laden Atlantic air, while northerly winds bring hot, dry Saharan air. Very broadly speaking, the south is forested owing to high rainfall and the north is drier savanna. Further north and into Burkina Faso, the Sahara desert is slowly encroaching.

A road journey from the coast to the north (about 12 hours by bus) shows this change in vegetation quite strikingly.

The most mountainous area is in the east along the Togo border, where several green peaks rise over 2,438 feet (800 m) to give an impressive view of Lake Volta. This is the largest artificial lake in the world, at 2,100,400 acres (850,000 hectares), fed by the White Volta, Black Volta, and Red Volta rivers and serving the Akosombo hydroelectric dam, which is 1,214 feet (370 m) wide and 400 feet (124 m) tall. It stretches almost two-thirds of the length of the country, with the equally impressive, lush Akuapem and Akyem mountain ranges on its western side. Ghana also has the largest crater lake in the world, the sacred Lake Bosomtwe, 19 sq. miles (50 sq. km) in area and 262 feet (80 m) deep south of Kumasi. The most heavily forested area is the rain forest in the far southwest, continuing into Côte d'Ivoire and beyond. The rest of the heavily built-up coastal strip is grassland extending about 25 miles (40 km) inland.

Administratively, Ghana consists of ten regions. The capital lies in Greater Accra Region, and Ghana's second city, Kumasi, is in Ashanti Region. With Brong-Ahafo Region, above Ashanti, these are the only regions to take their name from the name of an indigenous people. The others are the imaginatively named Western Region, Central Region, Eastern Region, Northern Region, Upper East Region, Upper West Region, and Volta Region. Each region is subdivided into districts, with a total of 138 self-administrating districts.

Ghana is a very fertile and rich land, particularly in the south, and is noted for its plentiful supply of yams, cassava, cocoa, rubber, maize, palm products, pineapples, oranges, papayas, avocados, plantains, bananas, and pepper, to mention but a few. Mineral resources are also synonymous with Ghana. It did not get its previous name, the Gold Coast, for nothing. Diamonds, manganese, bauxite, and timber are also found in large quantities. The 2007 discovery of large, good-quality oil deposits off the coast is due to launch Ghana into a new economic era.

CLIMATE

Ghana is hot. Although it's true that some periods and some areas can be cooler than others, even sometimes requiring a bedcover at nighttime, if you are coming to Ghana, prepare to sweat and take precautions against the sun. When the rain comes, it can be an awesome spectacle. It can also be very devastating, as the 2007 floods in the north attest. Cool breezes can be found on coast and mountaintop.

In general, the south (above the coastal strip) is more humid with higher rainfall. The north is hotter and drier. Temperatures reach 69.8°F (21°C) at night and up to 104°F (40°C) in the daytime. December to February is the coolest and driest time, and the time of the Harmattan, a red dust covering the sky as it is blown south from the Sahara desert. Then it's very hot until around April, when the first rains start, with two rainy seasons in the south (April–June and October–November) and one in the north (August–September). Global climate change has not bypassed Ghana, and what were once regular seasons are becoming unpredictable.

THE PEOPLE

Ghana's population is growing rapidly, and census results are soon out of date. Around 60 percent (and falling) of the population live in rural areas. The most densely populated areas are the cities of Accra, Kumasi, Sekondi-Takoradi, Tamale, and Tema. The literacy rate is 80 percent for males and 67 percent for females (2000).

Ghana is a nation that was created only in the last century, with very little regard for the indigenous people and languages within its borders. Thus, around fifty distinct groups are to be found in modern Ghana, each with its own dialect, culture, history, and traditions. To give an authoritative account of the people of Ghana would probably require writing around fifty books, and the author would have to apologize for not having sufficient room to allow the reader to appreciate these myriad cultures fully. All tribes speak languages from the widely distributed Niger–Congo group. As an introduction, we can mention the five major groups, each composed of smaller ethnic groups.

Almost half of all Ghanaians (47 percent) are from the Akan tribe and speak varieties of Twi (pronounced "Chwee"). Twi is also learned as a second language by many other Ghanaians and is considered the country's unofficial lingua franca. Akan customs can also, in most cases, be taken as being representative of those of the country. The Akans are thought to have emigrated from around the area of modern Chad in the eleventh century and now occupy most of the forestland in the south and center of the country. They include the

Akyems, Akuapims, Fantes, and Ashantis.

The Ga-Adangbe people (8 percent) who live in the coastal plains between Accra and Tema were originally from the Yoruba empire in modern southern Nigeria, moving west during the fourteenth century. The Ewe people (13 percent) also came from the same expanding empire in the sixteenth century and are now settled around the southern Volta Region. The Mole-Dagbani (16 percent) and Gonja people (4 percent) are the main northern tribes, who came from the north during the fifteenth and sixteenth centuries to dominate existing tribes in the area. Trade, particularly in gold, as well as expanding populations and empires elsewhere, were major reasons for this influx of people over the past thousand years. Scant information is known about the peoples living in the area before these migrations, or their fate afterward.

Stereotypical images of these tribal groups can also be made. A cocoa farmer wearing a toga of the brightly colored Kente cloth (shown on the cover), eating pounded yam and plantain (*fufu*) and drinking palm wine, is probably an Akan. His northern cousin is more likely to be a cattle rearer, wearing the heavy wide-bottomed dress known as a *fugu* or *batakari* and eating *tuo zaafi* ("TZ") and drinking *pito*, both made from millet. You are just as likely to see them both, however, wearing suits and speaking perfect English in the line at Barclays Bank. The Gas are renowned for never backing down in a fight, and have indeed produced some world-class boxers. In the south of Ghana, "Northerners" are often held in low esteem and can be the butt of jokes. However, they also have a reputation for being very hard and loyal workers.

Of course, in the twenty-first century, old tribal barriers are nowhere near as restrictive as they used to be, and people move freely throughout the country. You can hear Gonja and Hausa being spoken in the south, and Twi and Ewe in the north. Mixed marriages are common (apart from those between Christians and Muslims), and many of the current generation will tell you, for example, that their mother is Ga and their father is Fante, or they are half Ewe and half Ashanti. Such children will usually learn both parents' languages. The official language for all is English, and there is a strong feeling of "One Nation, One People, One Destiny," despite tribal and linguistic differences.

The population is growing steadily, and 2008 estimates put it at around twenty-two million, around half of whom are under sixteen years of age. From a traditionally agricultural, rural population, more and more people are now gravitating toward urban life. This gives rise to noticeable overcrowding and unemployment in the cities. A birthrate of 24 in 1000 and a death rate of 11 in 1000 is resulting in a steady rise in population. The infant mortality rate is 51 in 1000 and life expectancy is 56 years.

The Ghanaian Diaspora

Many Ghanaians live outside Ghana. Travel opportunities were seized during colonial times, and thousands continue to leave the country every year, mainly to North America and Europe for educational and financial reasons. These people are referred to as Ghanaians in the Diaspora, or as Diasporans.

Ghana is rightly proud of its famous sons and daughters in the Diaspora who have made their mark on world affairs. One of the most celebrated

examples is the former
UN Secretary General,
Kofi Annan. Others are,
to name but a few,
footballers (soccer
players) Michael Essien,
Tony Yeboah, Marcel
Desailly, and Freddy Adu;
Paul Sackey of England
rugby; three-time world
champion boxer Azumah

Nelson; Super Bowl winner Joe Addai; fashion
designer Ozwald Boateng; British parliamentarian
Paul Boateng; UK television presenter June
Sarpong and actors Freema Agyeman (*Doctor
Who*) and Belinda Owusu (*EastEnders*).

Of course, in the wake of a 400-year atrocity
that has seen many millions of Africans brutally
ripped out of their homeland, who knows how far
and wide the Ghanaian seed has spread?
Certainly, some aspects of Ghanaian cooking,
stories, language, and customs are direct
influences in parts of the Caribbean and America.
Many African-Americans bear striking
resemblances to modern Ghanaians.

National Flag

The design of the Ghanaian flag, the first flag

created for an independent sub-
Saharan African nation, is laden with
meaning and has since been adopted
and adapted by many of its
neighbors. It consists of red, gold, and

green horizontal stripes with a black star in the middle. Red signifies the blood of those who died in the country's struggle for independence. Gold represents Ghana's great mineral wealth, and green denotes its lush forests and farmland. The black, five-pointed lodestar is the symbol of African emancipation and unity in the struggle against colonialism. The national football team refers to itself as "Black Stars," and indeed any Ghanaian will do the same.

National Anthem
God bless our homeland Ghana,
And make our nation great and strong,
Bold to defend for ever
The cause of freedom and of right.
Fill our hearts with true humility,
Make us cherish fearless honesty,
And help us to resist oppressors' rule
With all our will and might for evermore.

National Motto
"Freedom and Justice"

A BRIEF HISTORY

The Republic of Ghana that we know today officially came into being on March 6, 1957, when the then Gold Coast gained its independence from its British colonial masters. Well before these artificial entities were created and mapped by the Europeans, however, the peoples of Ghana were part of a much wider, West African civilization.

Prehistory

Archaeologists still have much to discover throughout Africa, but discoveries so far, including evidence of toolmaking, farming, pottery, wooden canoes, and iron smelting, point to sedentary habitation of the area for at least the last 40,000 years, with the emergence of tribal groups at least 2,000 years ago. Long ago, the whole belt of southern West Africa was thick primary forest and the Sahara desert was much further away than it is now. It is thought that areas to the north and east of this almost impenetrable forest were populated first, with later migrations into the forest area as populations grew and competed.

Ancient Ghana

The first written accounts of the region by eighth-century Arab explorers describe the ancient empire of Ghana—"The land of the king" in the Mande language ("Ghana" being the title of the ruler). Situated 500 miles (800 km) to the northwest of modern Ghana, this is said to have been the first great West African empire, existing before the warfaring Islamic West African empires of Mali and Songhai that controlled trade and ruled over the various peoples of the area from the eleventh century. From the second century to the eleventh, ancient Ghana was a huge empire with a powerful military force and strong trade links to the north. It occupied land around the modern states of Senegal, Mali, and Mauritania. These ancient kingdoms were famous for their rich trade routes and for welcoming visitors from around the known world to their universities and luxurious palaces, at a time when Europe was wallowing in medieval squalor.

Some evidence, and much popular opinion, points to a migration southward of peoples from ancient Ghana to the area of modern Ghana, as a result of their refusal to be subjugated by these mighty Islamic empires and because of their wish to explore new resources and trade routes. This link was Kwame Nkrumah's inspiration when naming his new nation in 1957.

Tribal Groups

From the twelfth century onward, records show a settled population in what is now Ghana conducting an established trade in items such as gold and kola nuts with the fabled city of Timbuktu and North Africa. At this time, coastal trade from outside was unknown, but there were thriving fishing communities. Different peoples migrated into and out of the area during hundreds of years of war, peace, trade, and the establishment of tribal boundaries, to create a region populated by groups such as the Fante and Ga-Adangbe on the coast, Ewe in the eastern mountains, Ashanti in the central forests, and Moshi-Dagomba in the north.

In fact, all these cultures at the time mirrored the development of European states, where common ancestry, language, traditions, and not a few wars, had established agreed upon states and state boundaries. Had this ancient political system been allowed to remain and develop according to the will and needs of its own peoples, today's Ghana, Togo, Burkina Faso, and other countries would not exist. It would have been far more natural for states of Akan, Ewe, Frafra, and Nzema to have developed, just as political processes have shaped the countries of, for example, England, Germany, Spain, and Poland. Unfortunately, the economic desires of the Europeans did not allow Africa to develop along its own lines, and what we see now as modern African countries were simply carved out by Europeans. Thus, on that fateful day in 1471 when the first Portuguese seafarers landed on the shores of Ghana, a new, very disturbing, and world-changing era began.

European Contact

Trade was initially for foods and natural resources only, causing names such as Gold Coast, Ivory Coast, Pepper Coast, Grain Coast, and Oil Rivers to appear on early European maps of the region. Powers including the British, French, Dutch, Danes, Germans, and Swedes built a series of forts and castles, many still standing today, along the

coast to control the trade and protect themselves from the "savage natives." Ghana's rich natural resources and ease of access for ships meant that the vast majority of forts on the West African coast were built there. The earliest was Elmina, "the Mine," built by the Portuguese in 1482 to safeguard their haul of gold. Elmina is thought to be the oldest surviving European building outside Europe. For a while, the Europeans were content to exchange their guns, tobacco, alcohol, shells, and metal trinkets for Africa's rich natural resources. However, with the increased demand for labor in the American plantations, the sixteenth to nineteenth centuries saw the trade in human beings become the dominant global economic factor. The white man's guns were brought into the country in generous quantities, fuelling savage wars between tribes. The name "Slave Coast" appeared on the maps. The coastal forts increased in number and were filled with Africans, rather than African goods, destined for export.

The Slave Trade

The transatlantic slave trade made fortunes for the white slave traders and plantation owners, while brutally stripping Africa of its human resources. Europeans and Americans often argue that the slave trade had a negligible effect on the

world economy. Four hundred years and more than 50 million souls suggest a different story: the lucrative triangular trade was lining somebody's pockets. It is remarkable that the full story of this horrific trade is only just starting to be told in Western schools. Worse still, there appears to be no room in the curriculum for this era to be studied at all in Ghanaian schools.

It is true that it was Africans themselves who sold their countrymen into slavery by trading captives of war, that many (especially the Ashantis) grew rich on this trade, and that local chiefs allowed the Europeans to build their slave castles on the coast; but demand will always give rise to supply. Ghanaians accept the role their own forefathers played in the trade, but some maintain that they would never have participated to such an extent had they known the terrible fate of the captives. One Ghanaian language even has eight different words for different sorts of slave, showing that slavery was an existing practice before the arrival of Europeans. However, these "slaves" were mainly more akin to "househelps" who retained their human rights and ability to become free. Maltreatment of these servants was not allowed. Only those who had lost their human rights through committing a crime or had been captured in war were treated inhumanely and forced into slavery against their will.

It took nearly four hundred years, but the world finally woke up to the fact that human bondage and maltreatment were not nice things and, after a parliamentary campaign led by William Wilberforce, the slave trade (although not slavery itself) was abolished by Britain in 1807. Significantly, this was not long after the loss of her American colonies, which reduced the British slave market considerably. Other countries also abolished the practice around this time, although the trade still continued illegally, with various European slaving boats now turned protectors, patrolling the coast for human smugglers. The Africans had regained their humanity and stopped the drain of their human resources, but they lost a very lucrative trade as well, and income had to be generated by other means.

British Rule

In 1822, Sir Charles MacCarthy was appointed as the first British governor of the coastal territory, after a brief period of rule by British traders, who by that time had captured or bought all the coastal forts and castles. He felt the wrath of the tribes he attempted to govern, losing his head to the Ashantis two years later. It was not until the "Bond of 1844" was signed on March 6 (to become a significant date 113 years later) that the British colony of the Gold Coast officially came into existence.

This was a time when European powers were squabbling over which country could "own" which parts of Africa. This was known as the Scramble for Africa and culminated in the Berlin Conference of 1884–5, after which the map of Africa was divided up, with no thought given to existing tribal groups, into an unnatural jigsaw with pieces belonging to Britain, France, Portugal, Spain, Belgium, Germany, and Italy. Even after independence, these artificial divisions remain and are the cause of many of modern Africa's problems. The economic structures imposed by the Europeans were always designed to serve the imperial power, not the indigenous Africans.

Christians had of course been on the West African coast around the forts since the beginning of Africa's contact with the West, but it was not until the 1820s that a large-scale missionary operation began inland, first by the Bremen Missionaries from Germany and Switzerland, then by the British Methodist Missionaries and others. These were the first outsiders who wanted to provide something for the local population, not take something from them. They built churches, schools, and clinics and were the first to transcribe local languages, providing translations of the Bible in Twi, Ga, and Ewe, and writing the first Ghanaian language textbooks for their successors. Many schools and churches still bear the names of these early philanthropic organizations.

The original part of the country the British "owned" was divided into the Western, Central, and Eastern Provinces (now Regions). These names have been retained, even as seven more regions have been added to form modern Ghana. This is why Central Region is no longer in the center, and Eastern Region is no longer in the east.

Most contact so far had been with the coastal Fante people of the current Central Region. It is no accident that many modern Fantes have light-colored skin and English names. The colonialists found these people more placid and easily subdued than their northern neighbors, the Ashantis. No history of Ghana is complete, however, without mentioning the Ashantis or, to use the local name, Asantes.

The Ashanti Kingdom

Centered around their luxurious capital, Kumasi, the Ashantis' golden age began in the seventeenth century, when their future king, Osei Tutu, befriended a fetish priest, or *okomfo*, called Okomfo Anokye. At this time, the Ashanti state was made of smaller subgroups who, owing to their internal quarrels, were easily subdued by other states, most notably the Denkyira in the south. Okomfo Anokye is said to have received a

Golden Stool from heaven, which he used to unite all the Ashanti states under one king, the Asantehene. This unification gave rise to the largest, most powerful kingdom in West Africa, which grew rich through wars and its trade in gold and slaves. At its height, it covered most of modern Ghana, Togo, and Côte d'Ivoire.

The British considered the warlike Ashantis to be a threat to their activities on the Gold Coast, and fought a total of ninety-nine wars with them before finally subduing them and bringing them under the control of the colony. The last of these

wars was fought between 1900 and 1901. The Ashantis, already smarting from the exile of their king, Nana Prempeh, four years earlier, could not take the further affront of the British Governor Hudson, who arrived in Kumasi and demanded to be given the Golden Stool to sit on as their leader. This sparked a ten-month war in which the Ashantis, led by the Queenmother of Ejisu, Yaa Asantewaa, demonstrated their fighting skills before finally being outgunned by the Imperial British army.

Although they were ultimately defeated, the Ashantis' brave spirit and fighting prowess were much respected by the British. Indeed, Lord Baden Powell, the founder of the Scout movement and a soldier in the Ashanti wars, based much of his scouting teachings on the espionage skills and war strategies of the Ashantis. It is to the Ashantis' credit that, once they were made part of the Gold Coast, they embraced the opportunity to work with and benefit from their new colonial masters. If you visit Kumasi it is worth taking the opportunity to explore Ashanti history further in the museum or king's palace.

In 1901, the Northern Territories (now the Northern, Upper West, and Upper East Regions) were also annexed. In 1919, after defeat in the First World War, Germany lost all its colonies. German Togoland was added to the Gold Coast and renamed the Volta Region, and the borders of what is now Ghana were established.

Colonialism

The Gold Coast was a British colony for 113 years, from 1844 to 1957. The British, like all imperial powers throughout Africa, set about making money from the Gold Coast by trading in natural resources rather than slaves. Cocoa was established as the number one cash crop, and gold and timber continued to be taken out of the country in large quantities. The railways built at that time show where the British interests lay—tracks were laid from the ports to the

gold and timber areas and back to the ports. At one time there were up to eight thousand British administrators in the Gold Coast, all living in luxury on the back of these profits. Some frankly admitted that they opposed African independence because it would deny their heirs the same comfortable lifestyle. The fact that they had a

multitude of servants to cook their meals, drive their cars, clean their shoes, and even carry them in stretchers when traveling through the bush is one reason why the African notion that white people can't do anything for themselves has arisen. It also meant that African leaders craved power in order to enjoy the same luxuries and comforts for themselves, not for national reasons: this desire persists today.

It cannot be argued that the colonial administration did not do anything to help the local people. Roads, schools, hospitals, and infrastructure were built, agriculture and industry were developed, opportunities for overseas study were given, and a legacy of economic structures was left in place. But West Africans are proud people: they did not agree to the oppression of their people and the draining of their resources. By the 1940s, there were fierce calls for economic development, social welfare, and independence for the black man. Surprisingly, most modern Ghanaians tend to look back at only the positive aspects of colonialism, and any British visitor is welcomed as a long-lost brother or sister, whose ancestors "taught us everything we know," "colonial masters" being a term used with no intended negative connotations. Only a tiny minority hold a different view toward whites, and unsolicited shouts to tourists of "Slave master!" or "Babylon burn!" are not unknown.

Independence

The visionary freedom fighter Kwame Nkrumah, one of the lucky ones who got to study overseas, went to university in America and England from 1935 to 1945. (The first university in the Gold Coast was not founded until 1948.) Here, he was influenced by Marxist writings, which further fueled his desire to see his country free from the yoke of colonialism. His radical views had him thrown in jail by the British in 1949, only to be released and asked to form a government when they realized how strong his public support was. Nkrumah was one of the "Big Six" founding fathers of Ghana. As the head of the Convention People's Party, he uttered the immortal words, "At long last, the battle has ended, and Ghana, your beloved country, is free forever!" and Ghana was born on March 6, 1957. It became a republic on July 1, 1960. Ghana was the first black African country to achieve

independence. Yet, over fifty years later, Ghanaians are still asking themselves if they are truly liberated, as trade laws and economic inequality continue to put Africa in second place behind the developed world. For example, world prices of gold and cocoa are imposed from outside, it is far cheaper and easier for a Westerner to gain a visa to Ghana than vice versa, and the purchasing power of the pound and dollar far outmuscles that of the cedi.

Ghana's Leaders

Nkrumah did a lot for Ghana and is fondly remembered today. He built the Akosombo hydroelectric dam to provide power for homes and a large aluminum smelting industry. He built roads, the country's first expressway, and a deepwater harbor. He vastly increased educational opportunities within Ghana. He was also a leading light in the quest for African unity. However, power went to his head, and in 1966 he banned all political opposition, before being overthrown in a military coup and dying in exile. This was to be the first of four such coups in only fifteen years, as Ghana's leaders began to place their personal interests above the common good of the nation. Disillusioned with their leaders, the people of Ghana greeted each new government (and continue to do so) with a fresh wave of enthusiasm, only for their hopes to be continually dashed by corruption, nepotism, mismanagement, and incompetence.

The imposing half-Ghanaian, half-Scottish Flight Lieutenant J. J. ("Junior Jesus") Rawlings entered the political scene in 1979. His uncompromising military ways were not agreeable to all, especially the United States, which was uncomfortable with his anti-imperialist views and reputation for violence. He was even responsible for sending previous politicians, heads of state, and senior military officers to the firing squad for embezzlement and corruption while in office. Notwithstanding, he was still around in 1992 when his party, the National Democratic Congress (NDC), won the first democratic presidential elections held in Ghana. He served as president for two terms, until December 2000, and remains a strong presence on the national scene.

The next president was the "Gentle Giant," "Africa's Man of Peace," John Agyekum Kufuor of the NPP (New Patriotic Party), who took over the reins in 2000, and was reelected in 2004. Kufuor's reign of "Positive Change" was broadly appreciated by Ghanaians, although he left much to be done. He is held in high esteem in Ghana and beyond. In 2009, after a knife-edge election that was again fairly and peacefully held, although with voting reflecting tribal affiliations,

the NDC regained power under President John Atta Mills, a former vice-president of J. J. Rawlings. At the time of writing Ghanaians are still waiting for the NDC to fulfill their preelection promises.

GOVERNMENT AND POLITICS

Ghana is a constitutional multiparty democracy, originally founded on the British parliamentary model. Presidential elections are held every four years, and two terms is the maximum period in office allowed. There are currently seven political parties, with the NPP and ruling NDC being the big players. Ghana is a key nation in promoting political reform and respect for human rights in West Africa. It is a stabilizing influence in the region and is committed to helping resolve regional conflicts. President Kufuor was also the president of the African Union in 2007.

The government works closely with donor countries—the UK, the USA, Germany, Denmark, Japan, and the Netherlands—along with other countries, the European Union, and the World Bank, on programs to support aid projects and the decentralization of government services to local-level district assemblies. More than nine hundred nongovernmental organizations work in Ghana, mainly on welfare and development projects.

The legal system is based on English common law, but is also heavily sympathetic to African customary law. In fact, the British judicial, educational, ministerial, and many other systems are closely copied. These are not always appropriate in a tropical West African context.

Despite modern advances, and although Ghana is celebrated as being the leading political light on the continent, with the longest history of free

and fair democratic elections, there is still an overwhelming feeling that politicians are in the business for their own benefit, not for the benefit of the country. Discuss the country's problems with any Ghanaian, and you are sure to hear mutterings of "because of our leaders …" This opinion is well demonstrated in the very popular 2008 song "Our Money, African Money," by the Hip-Life singer, Sidney. If you can make sense of the mixture of Twi, Pidgin English, and French, this song sums up the public perception of African leaders very well.

THE ECONOMY

Ghana is a poor country, although in a much better situation than many of its neighbors. Foreign aid and remittances from Ghanaians abroad are heavily relied upon. Kwame Nkrumah's fifty-year-old vision of a self-reliant, manufacturing country with little need for foreign imports has not yet been realized. Incredibly, a country that produces cocoa and pineapples is letting them rot in the fields while importing Malaysian chocolate and Singaporean pineapple juice.

Ghana's main exports are cocoa and cocoa products (highest in Africa), aluminum, gold (second highest in Africa), diamonds, manganese, bauxite, fruits and fruit juices, and timber. Major imported materials are machinery and transport equipment, fuel, manufactured goods, chemicals, and food items.

Tourism is the third highest earner of foreign exchange and is a rapidly growing industry. Other major industries include hydroelectricity, brewing, aluminum smelting, furniture making, tuna canning, and chemicals production, but most of the population relies on subsistence agriculture. The productive agricultural and mining land all over the country is, literally and metaphorically, a gold mine for the nation's future, if properly managed. Another vastly underused resource is solar power.

Ghana's newly discovered black gold is being heralded as a resource to propel the economy to new heights of prosperity and growth. There certainly are large deposits of high-quality oil along the Ghanaian coast, but some, such as the maverick politician Kofi Wayo, are saying that Ghanaians should not allow the exploitation of this resource until they are fully ready to benefit from it. At the moment, estimates suggest that around 60 percent of the oil revenue will go toward paying the foreign companies and the loans used to locate, extract, and process it.

Although Ghana is a relatively poor country, it performs very well according to other criteria. The Human Development Index, which lists countries in order of wealth and quality of life, puts it at a lowly 135th place out of 171; but, more positively, Ghana ranks 40th out of 121 on the Global Peace Index and 29th out of 168 on the Worldwide Press Freedom Index.

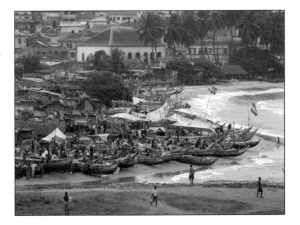

chapter two

VALUES & ATTITUDES

The secret to Ghana's peace and friendliness lies in the moral values of its people. These values derive from the importance they set on social harmony and the well-being of others, not just of the individual. This is manifested in the Ghanaian virtues of hospitality, kindness, compassion, generosity, faithfulness, and truthfulness, and their quest for peace, justice, dignity, and self-respect. On the flip side, however, especially where money is concerned, Ghanaians will readily complain of their own negative traits of materialism, jealousy, and corruption.

Attitudes of social conformity and tribal loyalty, which are firmly rooted in ancient tradition and religion, make for a tight-knit and respectful society with clear boundaries and rules, but Ghanaians also realize that such unchanging traditions can at times stand in the way of the open-mindedness required to accept and benefit from progressive, modern ideas.

Many Ghanaian values and attitudes can be summed up in proverbs from the local languages, and relevant examples are quoted here. Ghanaians use proverbs widely to impart wisdom, and being skilled in the use of proverbs is a revered quality.

Traditionally, Ghana has an oral culture in which stories, proverbs, and knowledge have been passed down from generation to generation.

COMMUNAL VALUES

Ghanaians recognize the dignity of their fellow human beings and have a deep and abiding concern for human welfare and happiness. Human relationships are considered the most valuable of possessions.

> *The human being is more beautiful than gold.*

Mutual help, collective responsibility, and reciprocal obligations are regarded as important. Observers of Ghanaian life constantly remark on their strong sense of community. Everybody in a community or extended family will know, and show an interest in, the affairs of everybody else. The idea that you could live next to a neighbor for years without knowing his name, as can happen in the West, is completely alien to Ghanaians. From birth, a Ghanaian is a social being who does not, and will not, live in isolation from other people. An unfortunate outcome of this communality is that it is a great breeding ground for gossip, and the "bush telegraph" will soon let the whole town know of any misdemeanors or scandals! Many proverbs teach Ghanaians that "No man is an island."

> *If two people carry a log, it does not press hard on their heads.*
> *A person is not a palm tree that he should be self-sufficient.*
> *You cannot tie a knot without using your thumb.*

In practice, this means that there are many ways in which people work together and help each other. A babysitter is never needed; people work together on communal labor or farming projects; wealth is shared; the elderly are never lonely or isolated; and a man will forsake half his evening meal and his wife's place in his bed should he receive an unexpected guest. The proverbial Ghanaian hospitality derives from these communal values. This is not to say, however, that this hospitality should be taken for granted; it does not allow for "freeloaders" who do not pull their weight.

> *Treat your guest as a guest for two days, and on the third day give him a hoe.*

These communal and reciprocal values are extended to the whole of humanity, not just members of a single community. Foreign visitors will therefore find Ghanaians showing an interest in their well-being and day-to-day lives, and will receive numerous invitations to meals, parties, or hometowns. Some tourists go so far as to say they find this intrusive, but this is certainly not how it is meant. To live up to the reciprocal nature of the society, visits, invitations, and gifts given in appreciation of someone's help are cherished as tokens of friendship and symbols of peace.

FAMILY VALUES

One outstanding feature of Ghanaian society is the emphasis on the importance of the family. It is not wrong to say that marrying and bearing children are more than expectations; rather they are requirements or obligations to society. Parents put a lot of pressure on their children to marry when they are of age, and do much themselves to find a suitable bride or groom for their ward. A marriage is the joining of two lineage groups, not just two individuals, and the two families are deeply involved in the whole process of finding a husband or wife, the marriage ceremony, and married life itself. It is unheard of for two individuals to elope or just walk into a registry office and marry. A girl's parents look for a responsible man with the means to look after their daughter and grandchildren. For a man, the search is always on for a woman who is of good character, obedient, hardworking, and well-respected in the community.

> *A good wife is more precious than gold.*

The woman must also be able to fulfill what is seen as her primary responsibility, the bearing of children. Inability to do this is sufficient grounds for divorce or the taking of a second wife. Modern medical tests are changing the traditional view that infertility is never attributed to the man. Childless couples are considered selfish and abnormal, or by some as victims of witchcraft, and do not gain respect or even sometimes a proper funeral.

> *Nothing is as painful as when one dies without leaving a child behind.*
> *There is no wealth where there are no children.*

As a result, large families are common, although not as large as in the past. Foreigners past their teens will often be asked straight away, "How many children do you have?" rather than "Do you have any children?"

Parents cherish their children and bring them up to be virtuous, respectful, and responsible. A brief glimpse into a Ghanaian home can give the impression that children do not speak unless spoken to, are sometimes not even allowed to look an elder in the eye, and are always either busy with their household chores or getting caned. This does not show the whole truth, which is that

Ghanaians love their children dearly and invest much time in them.

> *Absence does not bring up a child.*

Children are extremely respectful and obliging to their parents (and all elders). The unfortunate stereotype we have nowadays of antisocial British children, abusing and disobeying their parents and teachers, is unknown in Ghana. It is common for Ghanaian families living in the West to send children of a certain age "back to the village" to prevent them from becoming corrupted by lax Western values. Anybody in a Ghanaian community who witnesses a child misbehaving will have no hesitation in admonishing them, before dragging them back to their parents for more of the same. Children are taught to do only what is within their capabilities, and not to try to attempt something that only an adult should do.

> *A child can crush a snail, but he can't crush a tortoise.*

A child's family is much more than his or her parents and siblings. As part of a huge extended family, a child has the opportunity to learn from, and be cared for by, dozens of near relatives. It is not uncommon for a child to live with an uncle, aunt, or grandparent rather than his or her parents. Very often an elder girl will be "given" to a relative with small children so she can help care for them.

Members of the extended family, although not living in the same house or even necessarily the same region, see it as important to meet regularly. Visits are common, as are meetings at funerals, weddings, and other celebrations.

RELIGIOUS VALUES

Ghanaian society is intensely religious. Traditional African religion, or animism, long predates the arrival of monotheism. Even Ghanaians who are Christians or Muslims may retain certain animist beliefs.

Animist beliefs posit the existence of a supreme Creator God, who has intermediaries in his dealings with humans, such as spiritual beings or smaller deities who inhabit natural objects. God is considered to be everywhere.

> *If you want to say something to God, say it to the wind.*

A big reason why Ghanaians adhere to their moral codes is that God will know if you don't.

Things that happen in a person's life are given spiritual causes, and God will treat everyone according to the good or bad they have done in their lives. This proverb implies that nobody can hide their sins from the eyes of God.

> *Because God does not like evil,*
> *he gave each person a name.*

Traditional African religion is built into the culture of the people and is responsible for many of their beliefs and traditions. The Ghanaian cannot be separated from religion, and religion cannot be separated from the Ghanaian. God is

constantly referred to in conversation, proverbs, greetings, children's names, and explanations of natural events.

Thus, when the later, revealed religions of Islam and Christianity were introduced by Muslims from the north and Christian missionaries from the coast, a very receptive audience with similar beliefs was waiting. These two religions are now firmly implanted in Ghana, mainly retaining this north–south divide. Around two-thirds of Ghanaians are Christians, 15 percent are Muslims, and the rest retain their animist beliefs. Mosques and churches abound throughout the country, many with schools attached.

Churches attest to their European roots, Methodism, Presbyterianism, and Roman

Catholicism being major denominations. Pentecostal or "spiritual healing" churches have proliferated, as these offer an animated type of praise and worship more attuned to the traditional form. A Ghanaian will invariably ask you, "Which church do you go to?" rather than "Do you go to church?" Atheism and agnosticism are virtually unknown in Ghana (and are mainly confined to those who have lived overseas) and, for anybody wanting truly to assimilate into Ghanaian life, being a follower of religion is a must. If you are making friends in Ghana, these friends will sooner or later invite you to their church. Be prepared for long services, often only in the local language. For language learners, try to find one of the many churches that have one

pastor preaching in English, with another repeating
in the local language. Aside from the usual Sunday
morning service, there are Bible study groups,
prayer meetings, parades, and even all-night
services (known to be a well-used cover for
unfaithful partners!).

MORAL VALUES

> *The decline and fall of a nation begins in its homes.*

Tradition, religion, and strong familial and
communal bonds all work together to give a
Ghanaian clear moral guidelines, and the
development of a good character is considered
vital. Moral values are instilled in a Ghanaian
from birth, and can be divided into those values
affecting other people, and those values
pertaining to oneself.

   The ethic of responsibility for others is always
put above an individual's rights.

> *If you trample on somebody else's things while
> looking for your own, you will never find them.*

   Moral values are not necessarily founded on
religion, but on the quest for a harmonious social
life. Traits and actions detrimental to society are

considered evil in the eyes of both God and the people. These may include backbiting, egoism, selfishness, solitariness, laziness, lying, stealing, adultery, rape, incest, murder, and suicide. When Ghanaians do something good for another person or for society, they do it because they rightly believe that, directly or indirectly, they are also doing good for themselves. Sharing is expected.

> *If one person eats all the honey, he is sure to get a stomach ache.*

Similarly, actions against another person or society are likely to have detrimental personal repercussions.

> *If you don't allow your neighbor to count to nine, you will not be able to count to ten.*

A Ghanaian is expected to show respect to others, especially elders. This can be seen in the way people greet others. Insulting another person, especially using words like "stupid" or "animal," is immoral, as is not giving gifts or help where they are due. Positive character traits inculcated in Ghanaians include probity, patience, fairness, humility, gratitude, temperance, perseverance, trustworthiness, chastity before marriage, and faithfulness in marriage.

WORK ETHIC

Money is expected to be used wisely and shared among the extended family. Selfishness or wasting money on hedonistic pursuits is one of the easiest ways to lose respect.

> *Money is like a servant; if you abuse it, it runs away.*

Ghanaians are also very ambitious and, for the most part, hardworking.

> *The person who goes to fetch water does not drink mud.*

Any opportunity for advancement in the form of education, employment, or travel is eagerly seized. People will strive for power and influence.

> *If power is for sale, sell your mother to get it. Once you have it, you have the means to buy her back.*

In times of hardship, the Ghanaian values of spirituality, family support, sense of humor, and optimism can always be relied on to help retain a positive outlook on life.

Foreigners working with Ghanaians sometimes do not immediately perceive the work ethic of ambition and diligence, mainly because there is a very lax attitude toward timekeeping. Gender attitudes are also different from ours, and expats can expect to witness what they may consider very antiquated attitudes toward women in both the workplace and the home.

Westerners are generally viewed as having lower moral standards than Ghanaians. Social breakdown, warmongering, sexual depravity, marginalization of the older generation, and disrespectful standards of dressing and behavior all contribute to this view. Although foreigners will be afforded some leniency (an American in a miniskirt will attract fewer comments than a Ghanaian in a miniskirt), it is best to be aware of what constitutes acceptable behavior. Remember that you have been given the privilege of visiting someone else's country, and should respect that privilege. When in Rome . . . .

RESPECT FOR ELDERS

Older people are accorded massive respect in Ghana. It is believed that they have reached old age through living in harmony both with the ancestral spirits and with natural forces. They are regarded as the embodiment of experience, wisdom, and traditional lore, and their company and counsel is regularly sought by relatives. For their part, children and grandchildren see it as their unquestioned responsibility to look after their aged parents and grandparents.

> *Just as someone has looked after you when you were growing your teeth, so should you look after them when they are losing theirs.*

Watch how Ghanaian children address and behave toward their elders and this deep veneration is plain to see. Children make sure they greet elders correctly and may prefix every single sentence to an elder with the local equivalent of "Please." Ask a child a question requiring only the answer "Yes" and they will habitually answer with "Yes, please." It is not done for children to ask elders how they are, only to respond to the elders' questions. The younger generation should make a token effort of bowing, curtsying, or saluting when greeting elders, or of rising when an elder greets them and they are sitting down. In Akan, elders are often addressed as "Nana," which can mean grandparent or chief.

Even an elder sibling or friend is accorded the same respect. Firstborn children occupy a very special place in the family and much is expected of them, especially as regards looking after the younger children. The powerful influence of the elders is always felt.

> *When an elder is in bed, his feet are still outside the room.*

ATTITUDES TO MONEY

> *When you get wealthy, the people say, "You wicked person," and when you have nothing they say, "You unlucky person."*

Money talks in Ghana, and, unfortunately, traditional values can fly out of the window when cash is up for grabs. Attitudes toward a person are heavily influenced by how much money they have. Women will take gentlemen friends solely for their wallets. Somebody who is successful in business will encounter a lot of jealousy. Some people will attempt to emulate the same business, while others will actively seek to bring the successful businessperson down. People with little money will envy those who have more. (A Ghanaian who tells you he is "hot" is not complaining about the weather—it means he has no money.) Someone who is known to have money can be a target for unscrupulous thieves and armed robbers. Despite their seemingly happy and peaceful coexistence, almost everyone you meet will maintain that only sufficient money would bring them true happiness, and many are prepared to go to any lengths to get it.

Rich people in high positions may often consider themselves "untouchable" and abuse their power. In this regard, they would do well to heed the traditional Ghanaian proverb.

> *Instead of doing the wrong thing, then pacifying people with money, do the right thing and save your money to look after your children.*

There is often an element of the "pull-him-down" attitude when a Ghanaian is being successful (sometimes referred to as an African "PhD"!). This attitude, and the Ghanaians' idealistic view of European advancement and cooperation, has given rise to the following story as one explanation for African poverty.

A Self-Deprecating Tale

Two black men and two white men were being chased by a lion in the forest, and the only way to escape was to climb a tree. The black men started running, but one saw that his companion was getting ahead of him. Not wanting to be outdone, he knocked his friend down and reached the tree by himself. Unable to reach the lowest branch to climb up, he was eaten by the lion. The white men, however, ran to the tree together and were able to help each other to climb up, and were both saved.

PRIDE IN APPEARANCE

Looking good is very important in Ghanaian society. A morally upstanding Ghanaian is expected to dress well and make sure his or her family does so too. If a husband or children are seen dressed shabbily outside, then this reflects badly on the wife and mother. Especially for people of status, a smart appearance is considered a vital attribute.

Apart from the mad naked men sometimes seen walking about shouting to themselves, Ghanaians dress extremely smartly, especially for work, parties, and church, and much care is taken over personal hygiene and the washing and ironing of clothes. Women spend much time and money on their hair. Visitors should follow this example, as dressing inappropriately is a certain way to lose respect. Ghanaian women refer to a man as "handsome" because of the way he dresses, not his physical appearance. If you turn up to teach your first class in flip-flops, shorts, and crumpled T-shirt, maybe nothing will be said to you because you're from a different country, but you can bet they'll be muttering about you in the staff room.

All types of clothes are available in Ghana, including the cheap charity imports known as *Obroni wawu* (dead white man's clothes!). Buy some colorful local cloth and get yourself measured up for a smart church outfit. Wear black or red and black for funerals, and white for happier celebrations. Although it's seen all over the cities these days, with a style of provocative dressing known as *Apuskeleke* becoming increasingly popular, it is still considered unacceptable for women to show too much leg or bosom. If you are swimming, take a wraparound to cover yourself when you get out. Some elders do not approve of females wearing trousers; long dresses are better. For men, the unshaven look is not fashionable. Don't wear shorts when working or traveling. Remember that your appearance will directly influence the impression Ghanaians form of you. You may be a professor, diplomat, film star, or millionaire, but wear a T-shirt and ripped jeans to church, and you're nobody.

Good feathers are what make a bird beautiful.

TRIBALISM

Although Ghanaians have a strong sense of national unity, it is the tribe, or linguistic group, with which they feel most closely associated and which can dominate personal relations. One of the first questions asked on an initial meeting is "Which tribe are you?" and tribal links give rise to favoritism. Job offers, friendships, and political appointments can all be subject to tribal affiliations. President Kufuor, an Ashanti, made a strong unifying statement by appointing a Muslim from the north, as his vice president. Ghana's many French-speaking immigrants, especially from the poorer countries of Togo, Mali, and Niger, tend to be viewed as second-class citizens. People who live in a town, but are not of that town's tribe, often live together in a suburb known as "Zongo." Tribalism very rarely manifests itself as anything other than nepotism, except around Bawku in the Upper East Region, where clashes between the Mamprusi and Kusasi tribes continue to claim lives.

CUSTOMS &
TRADITIONS

In a country where ancestors are revered so highly, it comes as no surprise that traditions, established and preserved by the ancestors, are myriad, highly valued, and widely observed. Traditions, like attitudes, are changing with modern times. Some traditions, if carried out as before, would actually now be illegal or an infringement of human rights, or would stand in the way of development.

FESTIVALS

Don't turn down an offer to witness one of Ghana's many festivals. Aside from being lavish and

unforgettable events, they offer a link into the past and give an insight into disappearing customs and beliefs. It is no coincidence that tourist numbers in Ghana reach a peak around the major festivals.

Different regions have their own festivals and it would be impossible to list them all here. Many are thanksgiving festivals for the harvest of certain foods such as yams or rice. Others commemorate historical events such as an ancient war, the death of a respected chief, or the migration of people to their current homelands. Here are just a few:

Adae Kesee (varied, Kumasi)

The culmination of the smaller six-weekly Adae festivals (Adae Kesee means "big Adae"), this event celebrates the heritage of the Ashanti kingdom and allegiance to the Golden Stool.

Bugum (January, Northern Region)

A fire festival celebrated by the Dagbon, Gonja, Mamprusi, and Nanumba peoples.

Aboakyer (May, Winneba)

A deer-hunting festival where teams compete to bring a live deer to the chief. In ancient days a live leopard was required.

Dipo (May, Krobo)

A puberty festival to initiate young girls into womanhood.

Bakatue (July, Elmina)

A regatta to usher in the beginning of the fishing season.

Asa Fotufiam (August, Ada)

A warriors' festival.

Homowo (August/September, Accra)

A festival celebrated by the Ga people to remember a time when they were almost decimated by famine. Its name literally means "Jeering at hunger."

Agumatsa (November, Volta Region)

A festival to celebrate the spirit of the Wli waterfalls (the biggest in Ghana).

PUBLIC HOLIDAYS

January 1: New Year

January/February: Eid-ul-Adha, a commemoration of Allah's forgiveness of Ibrahim

March 6: Independence Day, celebrating the end of colonialism, with a big parade in Independence Square in Accra

March/April: Good Friday and Easter Monday (the most widely celebrated Christian holiday, even more than Christmas)

May 1: May Day, also known as Workers' Day

May 25: African Union Day, celebrating Kwame Nkrumah's launch of the Organization of African Unity in 1958

July 1: Republic Day (less of a celebration than Independence Day)

Moveable: Eid-ul-Fitr, the end of Ramadan, the Islamic holy month of fasting

December 1 (or first Friday in December): Farmers' Day, celebrated to reward the best farmers in the country

December 25–26: Christmas

WEDDINGS

Church weddings are celebrated in Ghana just as in the West, with all the same associated marriage vows, black tie, best man, honeymoon, legal recognition, and so on. Before this Christian tradition was introduced, however, customary or traditional marriage (a nonlegal but socially binding contract between two families), sometimes now referred to as an "engagement," had long been established. This is a custom that remains strong today, and a couple wishing to arrange a Western wedding will always have performed the customary marriage rites first.

As already noted, a wedding contract is entered into between two extended families, not just the happy couple themselves. Both families are heavily involved and have considerable influence over their wards' choice of partner. It is unheard of for someone to marry without their parents' blessing. It is even known for a man to ask his parents to find a suitable wife for him, playing no part in the selection process himself.

The dowry given by the husband to the wife's family is known as the "bride price" or sometimes "head money." This gives rise to the incorrect assumption that wives can be "bought," or made chattels of, in Ghanaian society. If a woman does not want to marry a man, she will not be swayed by any amount of money. The dowry can be fairly high, along with gifts and money to the wife and her parents and siblings, and many men cannot afford to marry young.

Polygamy, not approved of by Christians, is still practiced by some men in traditional society (notably chiefs). It is a very costly practice and one that can cause much tension between wives because of rivalry and competition for the husband's attention and money. Whoever cooks for the husband sleeps with the husband. Then it's someone else's turn the next day. Many husbands with only one wife regularly expose the African man's propensity for polygamy through their extracurricular activities. A married man *without* a girlfriend on the side can be seen as abnormal!

OUTDOORINGS

The closest Western equivalent to this ceremony is the christening or baptism. A Ghanaian baby from a Christian family may also undergo these Western ceremonies, sometimes as part of the "outdooring." The outdooring, as its name suggests, is the occasion when a new baby is taken outdoors for the first time to be shown to the community, traditionally on the eighth day.

An infant who dies before its eighth day is not supposed to be officially mourned, as it did not yet have an identity. A baby will usually be given at least three names, one of which is its "day name," according to the day of its birth. The baby is also given the name of a respected family member, and will be seated on the lap of this person if they are still alive and present at the outdooring ceremony. A name is also often given depending upon whether the baby is firstborn, second-born, and so on. The father may also give the baby a name with a meaning, dictated by the circumstances of its birth.

Many foreigners enjoy finding out what their names would be, had they been born in Ghana. The author, for example, could take the name Kwaku Manu Kaakyire, which means he is male, born on a Wednesday, and is the second and last born of his parents. The name Kofi Annan means a male, born on a Friday, and the fourth-born son. Whites, regardless of their day of birth, are often referred to as Kwasi or Akosua Broni (Sunday-born), perhaps because much of the initial contact with Europeans was at Sunday church services with the Christian missionaries.

At the outdooring, the baby will be given water to drink and told "This is water," then given wine and told "This is wine." The significance is to teach the baby to speak the truth at all times, and not (to use the analogy) to say that water is wine. Often a "cutlass" (machete) will be held over a baby boy, or a broom over a girl, to introduce them to the value of hard work. Gifts are given, speeches made, and everybody gets to hold the baby in between the drinking and dancing.

Akan Day Names

Find out which day of the week you were born on, and start using your Ghanaian name!

Day	Male	Female
Monday	Kwadwo	Adwoa
Tuesday	Kwabena	Abena
Wednesday	Kwaku	Akua
Thursday	Yaw	Yaa
Friday	Kofi	Afia
Saturday	Kwame	Amma
Sunday	Kwasi	Akosua

FUNERALS

Funerals can be long, lavish, costly affairs, and weekends can be taken over by loudspeakers, lines of plastic chairs, and people drinking, dancing, wailing, and pouring libation. Because so much reverence is accorded to the ancestors, Ghanaians give funerals a very high priority. Visitors may be surprised that such a somber occasion as a funeral can contain such high levels of merrymaking; but it must be remembered that funerals are a celebration of someone's life, not just a mourning of their death. "Real fun" is a very fitting anagram for "funeral" in Ghana.

It is believed that after death the soul of a person enters a spirit world, from where it maintains contact with the living and can protect or punish its descendants depending upon their behavior on earth. A funeral ceremony is primarily meant to prepare the soul adequately for this journey. The constant presence of the ancestors is the reason for the ample pouring of libations in Ghana, or for the shrines to ancestors visible in some homes.

A traditional funeral can last three days, or more for a notable elder. On the Friday evening the wake begins: the body lies in state all night to be visited by a long line of wailing mourners. On Saturday morning the coffin, containing some of the deceased's personal effects and other gifts, is taken for burial (cremation is abhorrent to Ghanaians, as they need to know that the body still rests in the grave for subsequent memorial services). After this food is served and speeches are given. There is an awful lot of handshaking as each new set of guests arrives. It is considered important to share a friend's grief and mourn together.

When someone is crying, your crying helps him.

Guests line up to pay their funeral contributions, which help defray the costs and support the family, and then have their names and the amounts announced to the crowd. The amount depends on the contributor's means and closeness to the family. Dancing and drinking follow. Saturdays in Ghanaian towns are often taken over by bands of drunk people in black and red, some of whom started drinking on Friday night and haven't slept. If it's a Christian funeral, there will be a thanksgiving service in church on the Sunday. Anniversaries of funerals are also celebrated, at one, five, ten, and twenty-one years. A widow may wear black clothes for a year after her husband's death.

Paying an excessive and unrewarding attention to ancestors and gross overspending on funeral celebrations are some of the customs that today's Ghanaians are beginning to question as the country adapts to modern times.

"RIGHT-HAND DRIVE"

One of the best-known rules throughout much of Africa, the Middle East, and Asia is avoidance of the use of the left hand. In Ghana, the left hand is used solely for holding one's toilet paper, and nothing else (except as part of a two-handed action). To give somebody something with the left hand is considered a blatant insult and must be avoided. If somebody *has* to use their left hand because their right is dirty, already holding something, or in the soup pot, they will support it under the wrist with the back of the right hand, or at least say "Sorry for left!" Never shake hands, point, gesture, eat, give, or receive with your left hand. This can be difficult to get used to—how are you going to buy something from a vendor, receive it, pay her, and take your change when you're both only using one hand? Coping stratagems include holding your bag open to receive the item before paying, offering a note held between your fingers to receive the item in your palm, or putting the money down on the table and taking the item in your hand.

CHIEFTAINCY

For hundreds of years before multiparty democracy was introduced into Ghana, government had been exercised by the chiefs of each tribe. Chieftaincy is far from despotism. It is,

in fact, a form of democracy, whereby the chief rules with the consent of, and in accordance with, the will of the people. Eligible men who will make good chiefs are elected by the people, who also have the power to depose bad chiefs. The royal family, from which the chief is to be chosen, and the council of chiefs of each state (made up of the subchiefs) are responsible for choosing a new chief from several suitable candidates; it is not the eldest son of the previous chief who is automatically chosen. Advisors, linguists (chiefs' spokesmen), and Queenmothers all make sure that the chief receives good counsel and does not rule autocratically.

> *There are no bad chiefs, only bad advisors.*

Traditionally, a chief is an amalgam of political head, religious head, judge, war leader, and advisor. Each has his own official stool (throne) of office, which is symbolic of the ancestral power he inherits when ascending to the throne. Paramount chiefs (chiefs of chiefs) will have many subchiefs under them, each bearing a name harking back to the time when a chief was the head of an army. Their affiliations refer to military formations such as the right wing, the left wing, the vanguard, and so on. Chiefs' palaces can be exquisite affairs full of cultural history; visitors are welcome to witness this for themselves at, for example, the Asantehene's palace at Kumasi or the Okyehene's palace at Kyebi.

After enjoying total power before colonial rule, the chiefs were also instrumental in working with the British under the system of indirect rule. The chiefs' power has been somewhat lessened today with the advent of national politics, but their status has not waned. Chiefs remain an influential force in local affairs, and even the president would be expected to show deference to the chief of his hometown. Chiefs also remain the rightful owners of their ancestral land. Anybody lucky enough to witness all the pomp, pageantry, and gold of a large *durbar* (traditional court reception) of chiefs will see the esteem in which they are still held, and the lavish attention paid to them. It remains customary to pay a courtesy call to the chief when visiting a new area. Don't forget to bring a gift of alcohol and/or money. A chief should not be addressed directly: all communication goes through his linguist.

MEDICINE AND MAGIC

Before Western medicine reached Ghana, medicine men, or herbalists, had collected a vast knowledge about local plants and their medicinal value. Even today, the forests of Africa are revealing more secrets in the battle to cure the world's diseases. Unfortunately, much of the old knowledge has been lost, and the decimation of the forests is making it less likely to be passed on to future generations.

For a more spiritual answer to health problems, or even for such ends as winning a football match, gaining the heart of a girl, or cursing an enemy, magic may be used. This is known as *juju*, and its practitioners are known as juju men. The juju men solicit the mystical powers present in nature to fulfill their interests, or the interests of anybody who pays their fee. A juju charm can be purchased that will protect its wearer from danger. "Witch doctor" is a term applied to a person who is a mixture between a medicine man and a juju man. His prescriptions are truly medicinal, but there is also a strong element of ritual and spiritualism in his treatment.

There is a strong belief in witches, who can take the form of owls when traveling at night. Bewitchment is a form of possession by a bad spirit, or the inhabiting of an object used or worn by someone by a witch's power. Witches may be blamed for causing sickness, accidents, barrenness, poverty, death, and other things. There is still a feel of medieval Europe at times, when a woman is accused of being a witch or when something bad is attributed to the evil power of witches.

FOLKLORE

Although the beliefs described below are referred to as folklore, any reader who discusses them with Ghanaians will find the strongly held view that these things are real, and will hear of many more.

One reason why many Ghanaians are scared to go deep into the forest is the presence of dwarfs, or *mmoatia*, who are more mischievous than evil and can kidnap people to live with them for several years before releasing them back to their homes. They are hobbit-sized people with backward-pointing feet.

The *sasabonsam* is another feared forest dweller, a giant bird who sits in the trees with his long legs hanging down to seize unsuspecting passers by.

Animals can be inhabited by the spirits of ancestors, making them sacred—such as the monkeys at Boabeng-Fiema and the crocodiles at Paga.

A person can turn into a snake. A snake can be made to vomit money to make its owner rich.

If you can stay in a sealed coffin for a week, you will become rich when you get out.

Legends about the origins of the tribes of Ghana are full of wonderful stories about coming out of a hole in the ground or falling out of the sky.

OUTDATED TRADITIONS

Some ancient traditions are changing or ceasing to be observed. Some were made illegal by the British colonial government, such as the practice of human sacrifice. This was most commonly done when a chief died, so that the spirit of the victims would serve the spirit of the chief in the next world. Today, chickens are the most common substitute, but foreigners are often jokingly warned to lie low if a local chief has died, as a white man's head is a prized ritual possession!

Other traditions are being questioned by Ghanaians themselves and are rapidly disappearing. These include the practice of *trokosi*, whereby young girls are sent to serve and live with a fetish priest (a form of soothsayer who communicates with the spirits), often as the repayment of a debt or family arrangement. Female circumcision, once common in the north, is now outdated. Betrothal of infant girls is much rarer these days.

Up to the mid-twentieth century, Akan law did not provide for any inheritance for a widow from her deceased husband, and she was often turned out of her home by the husband's family. This is no longer possible.

The old practice of domestic slavery, usually of prisoners of war, is now seen as a moral blemish in the Ghanaian appreciation of and respect for human life. Scarification, the cutting of tribal marks on an infant's face by some groups, is also becoming less common. Science and technology are replacing ancient religious and mystical beliefs.

DOS AND DON'TS

Everybody, visitors and Ghanaians, is expected to follow certain rules of etiquette, along with the values and customs already discussed. You can avoid faux pas by adopting the following practices.

- Do not smell food brought to you.
- Do not blow your nose while eating.
- Younger people should offer their seat to elders.
- Remove hats and sunglasses, and do not sit cross-legged, when with elders.
- Do not, at any time, cross your legs so the sole of your shoe is pointing toward someone.
- If accepting a drink of alcohol, pour a little on the ground as a libation for the ancestors before drinking.
- Do not point at anybody with your thumb.
- Don't ask for the toilet immediately upon visiting a house.
- Don't sing in the shower.
- Don't whistle at night.
- Never display any racist views.
- Don't speak disrespectfully of a very proud country and people.
- Swearing at or insulting another person happens, but visitors are advised to bite their tongues.
- Avoid kissing and intimate physical contact with your partner in public.

The significance of greetings, and knowing the correct responses to greetings, is probably the most important rule of etiquette that a visitor should learn about and observe. It is dealt with more fully in the next chapter.

chapter four

MAKING FRIENDS

The social circle of a Ghanaian is dominated by his or her extended family. Friendships are also made through living in the same town, going to the same school, working together, attending the same church or mosque, or sharing the same sporting or political affiliation. Home visits between friends are common, although it is more likely that friends will "bump into each other" outside. Social gatherings such as funerals and weddings are also regular meeting places where one can catch up with friends. Friends or family of existing friends are regularly added to one's social circle.

In the friendliest country on the planet, making friends is unavoidable. Social interaction, communality, and friendship are fundamental principles guiding Ghanaians' lives, and this helps to create a culture of warmth, safety, and peace. Loneliness or suffering in silence are unheard of to Ghanaians. From the day he or she is born, a Ghanaian is part of a family, clan, tribe, and nation who all have a responsibility for each other. Everybody knows their neighbors and the atmosphere is truly societal. Even outside the huge extended family, Ghanaians will open their arms in friendship to other human beings, in the knowledge that such a gesture will be reciprocated. The expression "If you do good, you do it for yourself" is a guiding tenet.

MEETING GHANAIANS

The workplace, place of worship, market, neighborhood, sports club, local bar, and the like will be brimming with locals wanting to associate with a foreign face. The issue is often not how to meet people, but how to find time to fit in all the people who want to meet you!

For a visitor who really wants to understand Ghana, know how to behave, and minimize hassles, a good friend is essential. Many organizations that send workers to Ghana arrange beforehand for a colleague, respected in the community, to act as guide, point of inquiry, and friend. If this is not done on your behalf, see if you can find one yourself. Ideally, this person should be of the same sex, employed, with a family, and not somebody who is always at the center of the town gossip. Ghanaians judge a person by who he is "walking with," and keeping bad company with drinkers, womanizers, or those unwilling to work, for example, will easily get you tarred with the same brush.

ATTITUDES TO FOREIGNERS

White or Asian foreigners are of course highly
identifiable in Ghana. Black foreigners may feel a
little less conspicuous, but non-Ghanaians are
quickly picked out by their behavior and
appearance, even before uttering a word in an
American or Caribbean accent. Your new
appellation (the local term for "foreigner") will
be *obroni* in Twi, *yovo* in Ewe, or *brofonyo* in Ga.
Many foreigners get fed up with the constant
shouts of "*Obroni!*" but Ghanaians do not, as is
sometimes claimed, intend any racist insinuations
by this.

If you are visiting Ghana, you will soon be
drawn into the culture of hospitality. Be prepared
for quite brazen approaches by strangers and to
be told, "I like/love you" or "I want to take you as
my friend." Taxi drivers, people in the street,
colleagues, and fellow drinkers in a bar can all be
your "very good friend" after one brief meeting.
The same applies when you introduce yourself to
Ghanaians. A Ghanaian will never be too busy to
talk, help, or give directions, and will never have
so many friends already that he can't squeeze you
in as well.

Despite the huge numbers of expatriates and
tourists in Ghana, foreigners are still a tiny
minority. Especially in the villages, the sight of a
white person can still have the local children
launching into song and following you around
chanting "*Obroni kokoo maakye, yaa fikyere
gongon!*" ("White man good morning," followed
by a nonsense phrase) and touching your funny-

colored skin, or running away in tears because they think you're a ghost. Even in the capital, where you can find whole bars or hotels full of tourists, you will still find yourself something of a novelty whom Ghanaians would love to get to know.

It is good to treat all approaches by Ghanaians as pure friendliness, as most are. However, the sad fact remains that Africa is poor and the West is rich, and, as a Westerner, you will be seen as having many more opportunities and much more money than a Ghanaian has. Therefore, you may find yourself subject to many requests for money, drinks, or gifts, often from complete strangers. Ghanaians may wonder why you would spend so much time haggling over small prices when you're so rich anyway. It's good to be generous, but the generosity of Ghanaians to visitors can be most humbling. If you are the one to invite someone out, you will be expected to pay.

ABOROKYIRE

Ghanaians who live abroad (which is known as *aborokyire* or "inside") are able to send money and gifts to their family and save for an investment when they return home. For this reason, a visa, especially to the USA or the UK, is a much-sought-after prize. The vast majority of these so-called "been-to's" or "boggas" (a corruption of "burger," the food these travelers are exposed to) have no intention of staying overseas for longer than is necessary. To them, Ghana is home, and the weather, food, people, and lifestyle are all better than those they experience when they travel overseas. Their travel is purely for financial reasons. They may have to do two or three jobs and abstain from many pleasures to get the money to send home, but many still seize the opportunity. Before taking a trip to Ghana, it is well worth looking up the Ghanaian community in your hometown for a briefing, and probably a few drinks. After your trip, you are sure to be eager to continue your Ghanaian experience, and they too would love to meet anybody who has been to their country. It is also very interesting to compare the views of *aborokyire* of those Ghanaians who live there, and those who have never been abroad. Look on www.africanchop.com for your nearest restaurant. A great Web site where you can discuss all aspects of the country with some friendly and knowledgeable Ghanaians (in Ghana and *aborokyire*) is www.ghanacommunity.com.

For those at home in Ghana who see the money rolling in from abroad, or whose friends return with money for cars and homes, the view of life overseas is usually seen through rose-colored glasses, with no mention of the unfriendly natives, terrible weather, and long working hours. This has encouraged huge numbers of people to look for any avenue to get abroad. Expect to be asked for a letter of invitation, sponsorship, or help with visa applications. It is very useful to have some prepared responses for people with such requests.

Photographs and anecdotes showing the more unpleasant side of your country, such as homelessness, unemployment, drug abuse, crime, racism, and antisocial behavior can help to dampen a Ghanaian's enthusiasm.

That is not to say, though, that foreigners do not regularly help Ghanaians to get to *aborokyire*, perhaps as a student, a worker, or even a spouse! If you feel someone has the potential to benefit from a stay overseas and you know and respect them and their background, then why not see what you can do to give them the opportunity? They are sure to be very grateful and hardworking.

SOCIALIZING

You will inevitably make some real and lasting friendships in Ghana, having used your common sense to filter out those with purely selfish intentions. You will also find that it is very easy to get to know Ghanaians, but difficult to get to know them well.

Visitors can develop hundreds of "acquaintances," but can struggle to find a true friend with whom they can share personal problems and deep issues.

A popular activity for friends is to go out drinking in the "spots." Some will invite you to their hometown, house, or church. A good day can be spent market shopping, cooking and eating with a friend, or taking a guided tour on a "tro-tro" (minibus used as public transportation). Ask a friend to come over to your place to give you some language teaching.

One peculiar characteristic of Ghanaians is that they will try to stop you doing anything for yourself. As already stated, colonialism has given rise to the notion that white people are so helpless as to require an entourage of serfs wherever they go to help them perform their daily tasks. Added to this are the Ghanaian values of helpfulness and politeness, making it very difficult for foreigners to carry their own bags, sweep their own houses, or cook their own meals (especially local meals). You may well get tired of hearing "Let me do that for you."

GREETINGS

Much importance is attached to greetings in Ghana. They are another way to show respect to your fellow human being.

> *If the person you respect respects you,*
> *you will respect others.*

If you walk into a house, workplace, meeting, or past a friend or neighbor on the street without saying hello, it is viewed as a direct insult. Much time can be spent in greetings before "getting down to business," and you should adapt to this.

If you enter a place and do not greet somebody you know on arrival, they can bear a heavy grudge and often refuse to talk to you until you

realize your omission and apologize. When approaching strangers for directions, or shopkeepers to buy something, there is a massive difference between "Good morning. Please, do you sell cigarettes?" and "Please, do you sell cigarettes?"

The general rule is that the person who approaches should be the greeter, so if you are sitting outside your house and a friend walks by, he or she should initiate the greeting. Of course, if you're walking past dozens of people every minute in central Accra, you're not going to say hello to them all, but do not forget to greet the people you know. Qualifiers such as brother, *bra*, sister, auntie, uncle, *ofa*, my daughter, *nana*, my friend, honorable, director, boss, or officer are often used when greeting, as well as the person's name. People love it if you greet them by name. A ubiquitous one is "Charlie," meaning "my friend." If your name really is Charlie, then you're going to think you're so popular in Ghana! It is not done to greet someone on the way to the toilet.

The benefits of learning the greetings procedure in a local language cannot be overemphasized. It shows respect, and leads to a remarkable level of acceptance from the people. There are so many ways of saying "Hello" and "How are you?" and greetings and responses to greetings lose so much meaning when translated into English. For example, ask an Akan to translate for you "*Ayikoo!*" and "*Yaa yie!*" "*Ayikoo*" translates roughly enough as "Well done," or sometimes "Welcome back from work," but "*Yaa yie*" can only be given the ungainly translations "Response to '*Ayikoo*'" or "Thank you for telling me 'well done.'" Another major difference in Ghanaian greetings is that your response depends upon who is greeting you. This incorporates the values of brotherhood and respect for seniors. Thus the English response of "Good morning!" does not allow room for the more meaningful vernacular, along the lines of "I respond to you, my sister / my partner / my male elder / my female elder." The Ghanaian English response to "Good morning" is "Fine morning." When somebody is leaving, a common valediction is "*Nante yie, wo ne Nyame ko*" (Farewell, God be with you).

HANDSHAKING

One's right hand feels ready to fall off from all the vigorous handshaking done by Ghanaians. A handshake in Ghana is much more than the brief, limp, token gesture we are used to in England and the USA. Both men and women do a lot of handshaking, although a "man-to-man" handshake is by far the more forceful. People may shake hands several times during the course of a short conversation, or indeed remain attached for the duration. Give a firm handshake, then slide down the hand until both parties are holding the other's middle finger between their middle finger and thumb, and end with a finger click. This may be repeated more than once. Also common is switching several times from the classic handgrip to the "thumbs-up" style and back again. If a member of the opposite sex uses their middle finger to tickle your palm while handshaking, then lucky you! To show some Rasta love, the fist-to-fist, fist-to-heart greeting is used.

When shaking hands with more than one person, you should always start from your right and move left, so that your palm, and not the back of your hand, is facing toward the next recipient. Even if you meet your very best friend walking with a complete stranger on his left, you would greet the stranger before moving to your friend. If you go to shake hands with someone who is eating or has dirty hands, they will tuck away their hand and offer you their forearm—just grasp it and give it a cursory shake. Two men walking together holding hands is a common sight and in no way a sign of homosexuality, which is taboo and illegal in Ghana.

TAKING PHOTOGRAPHS

You will of course want some photographs with which to remember your stay in Ghana, but try not to cause offence when taking them. There have been cases of tourists having their cameras seized, or even being attacked, for taking photos without permission. The best recommendation, if you want to take someone's picture, is to strike up a conversation with the person first, perhaps by buying something from them, and then politely asking if you could have a picture to remember them by. They will invariably agree with a smile, but be warned—they will ask for a copy of the picture for themselves! If at all possible, get extra copies of your photos and give them out if you meet the person again. Unless you are going to be very subtle about it, do not just whip out your camera and start snapping away. The other alternative would be to give camera to a trusted Ghanaian friend with a list of scenes you would like captured on your behalf.

Unless you've got plenty of disposable "dash" in your pocket (see page 84), do not get caught taking pictures of the airport, government buildings, Independence Arch, soldiers, or police. Avoid being caught taking pictures of the negative side of Ghana, such as people in ragged clothes, slum areas, or beggars: Ghanaians are too proud to allow you to portray this side of their country back home.

Accept a Ghanaian's invitation to their house, and you will find that one of the most common items in any living room is a photo album for visitors to browse through. This will consist of multiple deadpan photographs of the homeowner and his family, in various locations and types of attire. If you are sitting in your host's house, it is quite acceptable to pick up this or any other books or newspapers lying on the table. Show some interest by asking who is in the pictures and where they were taken. On the foreigner's part, one of the most popular items to bring to Ghana is your own photo album of your home, family, and country. Ghanaians will be fascinated to see what schools, houses, transportation, shops, and the weather are like in your birthplace.

GIFTS

Gift giving is cherished in Ghanaian society, irrespective of the monetary value of the gift. "It's the thought that counts" rings very true. Regardless of the nature of the gift, it is a symbol of peace and friendship. For family and loved ones, gifts are exchanged regularly. It is traditional always to bring a gift home after returning from a journey, typically bread. At parties, gifts will be given and received by guests and hosts alike. Ghanaians will often buy drinks, offer their food, or pay the tro-tro fare for friends they meet.

If you are arriving in Ghana from overseas, expect to be asked, "What did you bring for me?" on more than several occasions. You'll be hard-pressed to satisfy all 22 million inhabitants, but for friends, or those you'll be living or working with, try to bring at least a token gift. Clothes and toiletries are great, or mobile phones and MP3 players if you have the means. Presents for children are especially welcomed. Pens, books, sweets, T-shirts, balloons, and sturdy toys are cheap enough and can be shared between many children.

Ghanaian Joke: The Visit

Kojo and Yaw had not seen each other in many years, not since they left Ghana. They met in New York. Now they had a long talk trying to fill in the gap of those years by telling about their lives. Finally Kojo invited Yaw to visit him in his new apartment. "I have a wife and three children and I'd love to have you visit us." "Great. Where do you live?" "Here's the address. And there's plenty of parking behind the apartment. Park and come around to the front door, kick it open with your foot, go to the elevator and press the button with your left elbow, then enter! When you reach the sixth floor, go down the hall until you see my name on the door. Then press the doorbell with your right elbow and I'll let you in." "Good. But tell me . . . what is all this business of kicking the front door open, then pressing elevator buttons with my left, then my right elbow?" "Surely you're not coming empty-handed?"

Gifts can, of course—and usually do—come in the form of cash. The local equivalent of a cash gift is known as a "dash." "Dashing" also holds connotations of corruption. Ghanaians themselves regularly give money for funeral donations, weddings, political and sporting support, church collections, stricken friends or relations, beggars, and hungry children. Rich foreigners would be expected to follow suit, especially to say "thank you" to someone who has done something for you. "Blessed be the hand that giveth."

BEGGING

Most notably on some streets in Accra, the numbers of beggars can be high. Most are cripples, either being led by children or getting about on skateboards or hand-powered bikes and wheelchairs. These people, of course, receive no government welfare and struggle to find employment. Ghanaians periodically give to beggars, but usually just stare straight ahead when they approach the car window with their hand held out. Almsgiving is one of the pillars of Islam. Visitors can create a good impression, and help the needy, by giving something small to beggars, although children who solicit for alms should be ignored in order to discourage the practice. Pass money hand to hand with a smile and a kind word—do not just throw it to them on the floor.

VISITING A HOME

Foreigners will receive a lot of invitations to Ghanaians' homes. Very often, this will be in their faraway hometown, requiring any number of hours traveling in a tro-tro. You will not have time to accept them all. Inevitably, there will be some inviters with the hidden agenda of wanting to show off their white acquaintance to their family and hoping he or she will pay for all the bus fares and drinks. Use your common sense and others' advice about which invitations are well-intentioned, endeavor to accept at least some of them, and diplomatically decline the others. This will provide you with the best opportunity to get an insight into Ghanaian culture and family life.

There is a procedure to follow when being received as a guest in someone's home. The main thing for a foreigner to learn is to hold back with the small talk until this procedure is over. Although there will be some handshaking and chatting when you first arrive, the main event comes once are sitting with your hosts in the living room.

Take off your shoes before entering only if the person is a chief or notable elder. (Also, remove shoes before entering the sacred ground of mosques, shrines, or the consulting rooms of traditional priests.)

You will be offered water, which will be brought to you by a child or lady of the house on a tray. This is symbolic, and you should at least take a sip, even if you are not thirsty, and return the glass to the tray. The host, and possibly the whole household, will then shake your hand and say, "You are welcome." Say "Thank you" and, if the person is your senior, make at least a token effort of rising when they shake your hand. You will then be asked how you are and possibly how your family is. Even if you are dying and you have no family, the answer is always "Fine." The host will then ask of your "mission," i.e. the purpose of your visit. Then you can start talking. This is also the time for gift giving. If you have brought a gift of alcohol, it will probably be opened on the spot, unless your host has provided some already.

> *A meal to which one is invited is a delicious meal.*

You're not allowed to leave a Ghanaian's home without a full belly. A good host will arrange beforehand for your favorite food to be prepared, but whatever you get, be sure to obey the cook's order of "Eat all!" Not to do so can be taken personally. Don't be surprised if you are given a table to yourself to eat at, but you will usually eat with your host (if of the same sex). Ghanaians tend not to mix talking with eating. The typically British notion of an "uncomfortable silence," which has to be filled with some pointless chitchat, doesn't apply. To be together is enough.

It is rude to seek permission to leave too early, so don't accept an invitation if you know you have an appointment soon after. When you are finally granted permission to leave, your host will accompany you for part of the way. It is a strong sign of friendship to accompany a guest a long way. It is not unknown to be accompanied all the way back home, so your host then becomes your guest and you accompany him or her back home later. Sometimes the most meaningful and productive conversations can be had during these accompanying periods, rather than in the home itself.

Try to reverse the procedure when you are the one inviting Ghanaians to your own home—which should be reserved for close friends only. For the meal, regardless of how delicious your tuna salad or spaghetti bolognese really are, it is best to pay a Ghanaian lady to do the cooking for you. Otherwise, your guests will probably eat politely, and then go for *fufu* afterward. And don't forget to stock up with plenty of bottles of beer and/or spirits.

DATING

Ghana is a very sexually liberated country, although this is not immediately noticeable, because of secretiveness and the taboo against being openly affectionate in public. Before (and very often during!) married life, dating is common between Ghanaians. The word used for boyfriend or girlfriend is *alomo*. A popular alcoholic drink purported to boost a man's sexual potency before a visit to his girlfriend is Alomo Bitters.

More often than not, it will be the man who initiates a relationship. As well as the many women they meet through work, church, college, neighbors, and so on, Ghanaian men seem to have no qualms about approaching an unknown woman in the street or bar and declaring their love for her. "I love you" has a slightly different connotation from the Western meaning, and is more akin to "I fancy you." Nonsmoking and moderate-drinking men with nice clothes, cars, and money are the most likely to have their proposals accepted. Meetings tend to be furtive affairs, often in spots (bars), at home, or hotels. "Going out on a date," for instance to the cinema, a walk on the beach, dinner with friends, or a museum visit, is less common.

Apart from the "scammers" mentioned later, and those who (and whose families) see a Western partner simply as a source of money and a visa, relationships and marriages between Ghanaians and foreigners are commonplace and widely accepted. What is definitely not accepted, however, and what is darkening the perception of foreigners in Ghanaians' eyes, is the number of tourists seeking homosexual or underage sex. Homosexuality is practiced by only a tiny percentage of Ghanaian men and is well hidden. Lesbianism is also generally viewed with abhorrence, although it is more common, especially the practice known as *supi*, which is apparently going on up and down the country in the dormitories of girls' schools. The serious problem of Ghanaian men's enjoyment of younger women is humorously addressed in Mzbel's hit song "16 Years." (The legal age for sex is eighteen.)

chapter five

PRIVATE & FAMILY LIFE

THE FAMILY

The family is a strong unit in Ghanaian society and is held together by very deep bonds. All family members have roles to play within the family and also in their contacts with the neighbors and other townsfolk. Despite the many societal links, there is also private time within a nuclear family in which outsiders will not find it easy to take part.

A family in Ghana, however, is far more than the typical Western unit of parent(s) and two children. Everybody is part of a huge extended family, who, if not living together in a big compound house, meet regularly and take interest in each other's affairs. Accept a friend's offer to visit their home and you'll meet all kinds of aunties, brothers-in-law, grandparents, nephews, etc. The language used to describe the family relations demonstrates this strong bond; your sibling's children can be referred to as your children, your uncle as your father, and your cousins as your brothers and sisters. So don't be confused when your friend introduces you to two or more of his fathers! Beyond the huge extended family, everybody also has their place in a tribe or clan with similar bonds. The Akan society is matrilineal, and some other tribes are patrilineal.

HOUSING

Housing in Ghana is just as varied as the people, and it's impossible to describe a "typical" house. The proverbial mud huts are numerous in the villages. Some have wattle and daub walls, propped up with sticks, and leaf roofs. Other people can afford to use sun-dried mud bricks and corrugated iron. In the cities, certain areas are notorious for their slums. At the other end of the scale, you can see some magnificent, three-story mansions with ten or more bedrooms, a swimming pool, and all the modern conveniences. One family will go to the river for their water and the forest for their firewood, while another will simply turn on  the hot and cold taps and cook in the microwave or gas oven. By and large, town houses all have running water and electricity, if intermittently. "Light off" (power outages) remains a common annoyance.

THE HOUSEHOLD

In the traditional compound house, various nuclear families, individuals, or nonrelated tenants will live together. Most nuclear families (with an average size of five people) now live in their own homes, which are inherited, rented, or owned. Other relatives may also stay with them, either when the relative is in need, such as an elderly parent, or is offering help, for instance an aunt moving in to help look after her nephews and nieces. An older girl, not from the immediate family, may also be a live-in househelp. The frequent Western answers to these situations—nursing homes and babysitters—are unknown in Ghana and go completely against the values of respect for the elderly, responsibility for others, and communal living.

Children from previous relationships may also stay with their stepparents (a term not used in Ghana), and children from neighboring houses are free to play together or go outside. Half of all Ghanaians are children, and for the visitor, there's no escaping them when visiting a house. All older people are responsible for children in their midst:

> *It takes a whole village to raise a child.*

THE ROLE OF FATHERS

A father is the undisputed head of the family and his is the final word. It is his duty to work and provide money for the family, making sure his wife has enough for all the food and household bills. If the family owns a farm, the husband does much of the physical work. A father's relationship with his children, especially his sons, is strong and well disciplined. The male family members often eat in the main room without the females. The raising of children is a particular specialty of Ghanaians, favorably remarked upon by visitors, especially the love and attention given by fathers.

A husband is also expected to show interest in the affairs of his wife's family and to provide her with sufficient resources always to be looking at her best.

> *The beauty of a woman is due to her husband.*

THE ROLE OF MOTHERS

A wife's major role in a marriage is to bring forth children. Childless marriages can be seen as a curse, and a childless marriage is seen as the joining of two incompatible souls, and is not recognized as a "real" marriage. A wife's second role is to take care of these children, her husband, and the household affairs, and a Ghanaian housewife has more than her fair share of cooking and cleaning. A mother is expected to teach all these skills to her daughters.

This is not to say that the wife is always stuck in the house: many married women work outside the home as well. Familiar female occupations are hairdresser, seamstress, and trader, although there is no shortage of female lawyers, politicians, head teachers, and professors as well. Nor do women take a back seat in the nation's

affairs. Queenmothers are highly influential figures in the chiefs' palaces, and 80 percent of the trading activities in the country are controlled by the jolly, business-savvy "Market Mammies."

GROWING UP IN GHANA

Children are raised to be respectful to their parents, hardworking, and serious about their

education. It sometimes seems that all their out of school hours are spent helping in the home or family business, or out on the streets selling things. An eldest daughter is expected to be able to do all the same chores as her mother by her early teens. There is time for play, though, and kids fill this time with football, television, board games, and dancing games such as *ampe*. The time-honored entertainment for children is to sit round the elders in the evening and be enthralled and educated by traditional folktales, especially about the cunning but greedy spiderman, Kwaku Ananse (see page 118). The elders take the care and upbringing of children very seriously.

> *When the old woman is hungry, she says, "Cook something for the children to eat."*

There is never the problem of a shortage of playmates, or of parents not allowing their children to play outdoors. Unfortunately, reading and writing for pleasure do not figure highly on a Ghanaian child's agenda.

Education

> *When a yam doesn't grow well, we don't blame it: it is because of the soil.*

Education in Ghana is highly valued and students are diligent and immaculately well behaved, but the system has one big problem: children are not taught to think for themselves, but are rather taught in a didactic, rote-learning fashion that does nothing to help develop inquiring young minds. There is an emphasis only on remembering by heart the "correct" answer, to be regurgitated upon the teacher's command. Learning is evaluated by the teacher asking, "Understand?" followed by a chorus of "Yes, Sir!" or "Yes, Miss!" whether the pupils understand or not. A typical example is that of a schoolboy who

was asked what he had learned today. "We did addition," came the answer. "OK, what's twelve plus fifteen?" "I don't know—our teacher didn't tell us that one." A teacher's lesson plan looks more like a play script, consisting of a long list of "teacher's questions" and "pupils' expected responses."

Even in secondary and higher education, students can be found whose sole desire is to memorize as much "big English" as possible in order to write it down verbatim in exams, without necessarily understanding or being able to apply it. Also, education in Ghana still owes much to its colonial roots, and some teaching resources have not changed since colonial times, so children can be found reading about the British seasons, studying British maps, and learning about British animals that they have never encountered.

To its credit, the Ghana Education Service has recognized these drawbacks and comprehensive education reforms were put in place in 2008, in order to offer a more relevant curriculum with increased pupil participation. Teachers' poor salaries, however, continue to give the profession a low status. Many schools have very limited resources. A recent survey suggested that more than 50 percent of teachers regularly fail to show up at their classrooms; many of them are working in second jobs.

Primary education (which is compulsory, mainly free, and available to all) lasts for six years. Children then enter a junior high school for four years and a senior high school for four years. The option then for the lucky few is to enter a university, a technical college, or a teacher training college. Graduates are required to perform at least one year of National Service in a government institution.

DAILY LIFE

Sunrise in Ghana is always just before 6:00 a.m., but households up and down the country are awakening, cocks crowing, and gospel music playing well before then. Visitors living with a host family or in a built-up area should not expect to sleep in. Early morning is the best time to get things done before the sun gets too fierce. Sweeping the compound and washing clothes by hand are early morning chores for women or older children. Schools can start by 7:00 a.m., so children have to be fed, bathed, and dressed in good time.

Traditionally, the man leaves for work and the woman takes care of the housework for some time before eating a late breakfast or an early lunch. The hot afternoon often gives time for a siesta before continuing work when the sun's heat has died down. Going to the market and preparing the evening meal can take some hours. Daily shopping for fresh produce is usually done at an open-air market, with larger supermarkets and smaller kiosks stocking other nonperishable goods. A great example of the modernization of shopping in Ghana is the huge Accra Mall, opened in 2007. The day is also, of course, filled with many visits and greetings.

The sun falls out of the sky just after 6:00 p.m., and it is around this time that the main meal is served. Television, church, or going out for a walk or a drink occupy the last few hours before an early bedtime. People tend to bathe twice a day. Bucket baths are the norm, using a "sponge" that isn't a sponge but a long strip of netting. Saturdays can be taken over by funerals, and Sundays by church.

HEALTH CARE

Most big towns have hospitals or clinics for serious cases of illness. Hospital treatment used to be an expensive affair beyond the means of many townsfolk, but the government is now being highly praised for the introduction in 2004 of the National Health Insurance Scheme (NHIS). Now, for an annual payment of around US $10, patients receive all required health care under the scheme. This should be borne in mind if you are contacted by "scammers" claiming they need hundreds of dollars for their sick mother's hospital fees.

For lesser complaints, Ghanaians self-prescribe and pick up medicines at smaller drugstores (not covered by the NHIS), or go down the route of spiritual or traditional healing. Examples of natural remedies are tea made from the leaves of the neem tree and pepper soup (*nkrakra*) to alleviate fevers.

chapter six

TIME OUT

Ghanaians have a lot of leisure time, love socializing, and do this in a very relaxed and informal way, often just sitting by the roadside and watching life go by, without feeling the need to "go out and do something together." There is a different and much more laid-back attitude toward time and work than in many developed countries, making opportunities for socializing numerous and inherent in daily life. Socializing may be done in large groups or between just two people. A visitor with a good friend and time on his or her hands will be spoiled for choice for attractions to visit and things to do. Very often, the most enlightening experiences don't require huge expenditure and travel; it can all happen just on your doorstep.

EATING OUT

It is quite possible, if you are so inclined, to live on an entirely Western diet in Ghana. Your hotel can start you off with a full English or continental breakfast before you go out to sample some of the many French, Chinese, Lebanese, and

Italian restaurants. Supermarkets stock a full range of imported foods.

For those preferring to cook for themselves, the bounty of Ghana's rich farmland provides a fresh, organic, healthy diet. Delicious fruits and vegetables are widely available and cheap. Fish and meat can be eaten on the day of slaughter, or kept fresh in cold stores. The main breads available are sugar, butter, and tea bread. Try to use local ingredients wherever possible (e.g. Ghanaian, not American rice).

To really understand Ghanaian foods and cooking, however, visitors are recommended to roll up their sleeves and enjoy the experiences of, for example, pounding *fufu*, "driving" (stirring) *banku*, grinding pepper in an earthenware pot instead of a

blender, lighting and fanning the coal pot, or slaughtering the chicken, goat, or cow. A favorite orientation activity for newcomers is a trip around a local market, followed by cookery practicals. Popular foods among tourists include red-red (fried plantain with bean stew), *jollof* rice (rice cooked in a meat and vegetable stew), *waakye* (spiced rice and beans), rice balls with groundnut (peanut) soup, *borfrot* (doughnut), *mpotompoto* (mashed yam with palm oil and fish), *kelewele* (spiced fried plantain), and the fresh fish, shrimps, and "one-man-thousand" (tiny fried baby fish—one man can eat a thousand of them) straight from the Volta around Akosombo.

A day out with a cocoa or plantain farmer, palm-wine tapper, grasscutter (cane rat) rearer, cattle herder, or maize grinder can be an enjoyable and culturally informative experience. Many Ghanaians have their own subsistence farms at home, or at least a few fruit trees. Any visitor staying for a period of years could even try to start their own small farm. This would also help to

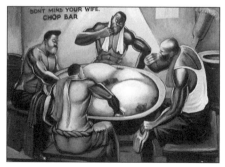

break the myth that white people can't do anything.

"Chop" is Ghanaian English for food, or to eat, and the local food is served in the ubiquitous chop bars. Food in chop bars is served hot, quickly, and cheaply. *Fufu*, which is swallowed without chewing, is notoriously difficult to eat for first timers. The other two big local dishes are *kenkey* (*dokono*) and *banku*, made from maize flour. Regional delicacies abound; a few of them are described below.

NAME OF FOOD	INGREDIENTS	REGION
nkran dokono	Fermented maize in maize leaves	Greater Accra
fante dokono	Fermented maize in plantain leaves	Central
akyeke	Cassava	Western
akple ("banku's brother")	Maize	Volta
ampesi	Boiled yam or plantain	Eastern, Brong-Ahafo
fante fante	Palm oil and fish	Central
koko with koose	Millet or maize porridge with fried bean balls	Northern, Upper West, Upper East
tubaani	Bambara beans	Northern, Upper West, Upper East
tuo zaafi ("TZ")	Millet	Northern, Upper West, Upper East

ETIQUETTE

The etiquette of eating is an important lesson visitors should learn. The right hand must be washed before eating. Most foods are eaten with the hands, but nobody will mind if you request a spoon. Very often, two or more people will share a meal from the same bowl and this can be a very bonding experience.

Ghanaians tend to eat very fast, and the fussy foreigner taking his time to chew his food well and provide light conversation will be told, "Why? Eat! You are not eating!" There is pride to be had in gaining the "Gold Medal," or being the last one at the pot after your eating companions have all retired with full bellies.

"You are invited" is said by someone who is eating when you approach them. It is usually a perfunctory offer, but may be accepted (wash your hands first!). If you are the one eating and you do not invite those around you, they will be offended, even if they have no intention of accepting your invitation. Belching after a big meal should be avoided, unless you want to gain the accolade of "Bush Boy" or "Bush Girl."

Traditionally, men and women do not eat together, sometimes not even in the same room. It is not done to eat while walking. If you are eating something bigger than bite-size, it is more acceptable to break pieces off with your hand rather than put the whole thing in your mouth and bite it.

DRINKING

"Going for a few bottles" is a pastime of many Ghanaians. Even for teetotalers, sitting down with some friends at one of Ghana's many "spots," chatting, listening to the music, and watching life go by is a common way to spend one's free time.

Even the nation's favorite beer, Star, is used as an acronym for "Sit Together And Relax." Spots come in a variety of forms, all usually noticeable by colored vertical stripes or big drinks logos on the front. That is, if you don't notice the loud music and drunk people first. Some spots can be smaller than your living room and serve only local drinks, usually *akpeteshie*, which is strong gin distilled from palm wine. The undistilled palm wine is much more refreshing and less likely to kill you—look out for a white flag on the country roads. *Pito* and *zom koom* are popular drinks in the north, made from millet. Most spots are bigger and serve bottled drinks such as lager (Star, Club, Stone), Guinness, Castle Milk Stout, fizzy drinks, known as "minerals" (Coke, Fanta, Sprite), fruit juices (a fruit juicer is a great present to bring over), and "malt," which, like Marmite, you will either love or hate. It actually tastes a bit like Marmite, too. At the top end of the scale, there are numerous nightclubs, pool halls, casinos, and concert halls, all serving drinks.

Spots can be great places to meet friends and to make new ones. They are also often used for lovers' meetings, and sometimes have specially designed "hiding places." Food can be bought and eaten in spots, either from the spot itself, the nearby stores, or a passing vendor. The common "hissing" used to attract someone's attention, followed by "banana seller!" / "meat-pie seller!" / "kebab seller!" / "popcorn seller!" is a common sound in the spots. Music and dancing are the norm.

Lots of Ghanaians drink. Some Ghanaians drink a lot. Normally unreserved anyway, a Ghanaian who has "downloaded some hot one" will often seize you and refuse to let you stop talking to him. *Akpeteshie* bars during happy hour (that is, any hour) can be funny places full of strong opinions and strange behavior, but don't make a habit of frequenting them, for the sake of your own reputation. At all times be aware that a white person is very conspicuous in Africa, and you do not want to develop a negative reputation as a drinker. By all means drink your head off every evening if that's your bag, but try to do it out of the public eye as much as possible. Alcohol abuse is known as "the white man's disease" in Africa and expats should be careful to not make drinking the only "time out" they take.

SMOKING

Cigarettes in Ghana are known as "jot." They are cheap, come in many brands, and can be sold individually. They are sold in some kiosks, by cigarette vendors, and in bars. Smoke them either where you buy them or in your house. Do not walk the streets with a cigarette.

Smoking is not respected at all in Ghana, and if you are a smoker, you are well-advised to hide it. Among women, smoking is reserved for prostitutes. A strange but widespread belief among Ghanaians is that foreigners tend to smoke a lot because it helps them to keep warm in their cold countries.

Marijuana, known as "wee," is also cheap and common. Wee smokers, however, are given probably the lowest respect of all, and wee smoking is an illegal and unacceptable practice. Ghana's prisons have their fair share of foreign drug offenders who are given no bail, no repatriation, and no sympathy.

MUSIC

Music plays a huge role in Ghanaian society and can always be heard in the big towns, often at incredible decibel levels. The constant tunes coming from bars, parties, radio and television, and private homes and cars are

impossible to escape. Ghanaian music is some of the most enjoyable and beautiful music you will ever hear, and can be appreciated even with no clue as to what the songs are about (although many of them are sung in English). Of course, if you find a song you like, you will inevitably want to know what they're singing, and music is therefore a very good language learning tool. Most music you hear not in English will be sung in Twi.

The oldest, most traditional music in Ghana is the ageless African rhythm of drumming and dancing, which continues to entertain crowds today. It is also common to see traditional instruments still being used: you may see xylophones, gongs, bells, rattles, cattle bells, clappers, *prempensua* (African piano), gourds, horns, trumpets, and flutes. Traditional regional styles include Kpanlogo (Ga), Simpa (Dagomba), Bosue (Akan), and Borborbor (Ewe). Later came Palm Wine Music, influenced by visiting sailors, which is sung by old men in local languages accompanied by a battered guitar and any available wood or metal percussion instruments. Kwabena Nyama was one of its foremost practitioners. Church music is lively, lengthy, and loud.

Traditional African sounds fused with jazz and soul influences during the colonial period of the Gold Coast to form High-Life music, so called because it was originally performed at lavish functions for the ruling British elite; those enjoying the "high life." Popular High-Life musicians include A.B. Crentsil, Abrantie Amakye Dede (owner of the famous Abrantie Spot in Accra), Daasebre Gyamena, Daddy Lumba, and Kojo Antwi. Bogga (or Burger) High-Life is a variation of this with European influences, originating from such artists as George Darko, who had emigrated to Germany.

In the early 1990s, Reggie Rockstone was the first artist credited with mixing High-Life with American Hip-Hop, to create Hip-Life music, which has developed into a thriving international movement, very popular with the younger generation. There are many talented Hip-Life artists, including Batman, Castro Destroyer, Kwabena Kwabena, Obrafour, Praye, Ofori Amponsah, and Tic-Tac. Hip-Life is also proving

to be a successful breeding ground for many up-and-coming female artists, most notably the incredible Mzbel. Female singers had previously been limited to the inescapable Gospel music, Cindy Thompson, Esther Smith, the Tagoe Sisters, and Daughters of Glorious Jesus being popular performers. For some great Ga music that's sure to get you on your feet, keep an ear out for King David. Reggae is developing through artists such as Rocky Dawuni, Shasha Marley, and Blakk Prophet. Reggae fans will appreciate the music and message of Blakk Rasta daily on Hitz FM, and his catchy tribute to Barack Obama.

Other African music is commonly heard. Selected continental anthems include "African Queen" by 2Face of Nigeria, "Premier Gaou" by Magic System, or anything by Alpha Blondy of Côte d'Ivoire, "Agolo" by Angelique Kidjo of Benin, and songs from the South African "kwaito-

cum-marabi house music" band, Mafikizolo.
There are Bob Marley fans aplenty. Say a prayer as
you listen to anything by the late, great king of
African Reggae, Lucky Dube, who was so sadly
stolen from us in October 2007, a victim of the
situation in the troubled South Africa—the very
issue that he addressed through his powerful
lyrics and Rastafarian message. His tracks are to
be heard everywhere, and the reaction to his
murder by armed robbers has been massive and
heartfelt throughout Africa.

TIPPING

Tipping—that is, paying something extra for
a service, and to be differentiated from
"dashing"—is not a practice commonly observed
by Ghanaians. They will rather total their bill
carefully and demand the exact change.

However, at the tourist sites where you have a
guide, such as the chiefs' palaces, game reserves,
and slave castles, the guide will expect a tip.
Guides consistently provide excellent service,
enough to warrant a tip. Be careful not to pick
up any "fake" guides, who will follow you
around, provide no service, then demand a tip
for services you haven't even asked for.

Waiters and waitresses, hotel workers, and bar
staff do not usually expect a tip, but for good
service, a small gratuity, a "Keep the change" or
"Have a drink on me" is good practice.

SHOPPING FOR PLEASURE

An instantly noticeable source of shopping in Ghana is the "hawkers" who line the streets and pavements shouting their product and its price.

You can buy anything on the streets, from ice cream to puppies, and one of the best ways to shop is from the comfort of your car or tro-tro. The streets of Accra have been dubbed "the longest supermarket in the world." The hawkers in the traffic seem to have the hardest job, running after potential customers in the hot sun and narrowly avoiding death when the lights change to green.

Tro-tro shopping is a highlight of many a visitor's stay in Ghana. Many other goods are sold in supermarkets and smaller stores.

Haggling

Ghanaians haggle over prices, but not in all circumstances. Shops, hotels, meals, and drinks usually have fixed prices, but most items bought on the street and hired taxis can be subject to lengthy bartering. When buying foodstuffs, you can try your luck by asking for a reduction in price (*te so*) or for the addition of some free extras (*to so*). A Ghanaian friend with you when you shop will ensure you don't pay too much, as many prices quoted initially by the seller can be reduced by half.

Ask them if they are charging you *obroni* price or *obibini* (Black man) price. By all means haggle, but do not insult or cause offense. If you don't want to waste your time bartering and are happy to contribute to the economy of Africa, just ask the seller for his or her "last price" and pay that.

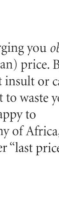

Souvenirs

Arts and crafts shopping is an interesting pastime, and you can find some great presents to take home. Ghanaian art is filled with symbolism and offers insights into the history and beliefs of the people. Accra Arts Centre has a wonderful array of local crafts at wonderfully inflated prices (which do need to be haggled for!) Drums, masks, sculptures, swords, bows, pottery,

beads, fabrics, and paintings are plentiful. Locally, go for some Kente or Adinkra cloth or Ashanti gold weights from Kumasi, woven hats and baskets in the north and east, a traditional smock (*batakari*) with matching trousers and hat from Bolgatanga, or a coffin in the shape of a fish, beer bottle, coconut, or anything you request from Teshie Nungua.

TOURISM

Besides Ghana's main tourist attraction, namely its incredible people, the country has a wide gamut of sites of interest to tourists. European forts and castles are now museums or hotels; lake, river, and beach resorts are offering water sports and game fishing; national parks are developed and well managed; facilities are available for large social gatherings, and more nature, adventure, and ecotourism packages are being offered in the remaining forests.

The Ghana Tourist Board provides an excellent service and will give you much more detailed information on all their popular tourist sites and possible itineraries. For readers of this book who are interested in developing their knowledge of the culture and customs of Ghana, the following places or activities are specifically recommended.

CBEP

The Community-Based Ecotourism Project has developed fourteen rural locations in consultation with tourists, in order to alleviate poverty through the creation of income-generating tourism activities. For example, there are protected areas including butterfly, monkey, hippo, crocodile, and bird-watching sanctuaries, and villages have been turned into pottery and art workshops. Visitors to these sites will have a great opportunity to learn deeply about the people and their lifestyles, in the knowledge that their tourist dollars are going directly toward the community.

Akyem Abuakwa

This ancient kingdom, now part of the Eastern Region, has the potential to become one of the biggest tourist hubs in the country. Ironically, perhaps one of its main pulls is the fact that it has yet to achieve this potential. One can freely roam among the lush hills, waterfalls, sacred caves, ancient shrines, artificial lakes, butterfly and monkey sanctuaries, and giant trees. Traditional beliefs and ways of life are pursued by a proud people who welcome foreigners keen to learn about them.

Kumasi

The Ashantis are rightly proud of their rich history, and the visitor will find no shortage of museums and cultural and historical sites in the area to impart this (and also the biggest market in West Africa). Ashantis consider themselves the purest of Akans and a study of their culture is highly recommended. An educated Ashanti will give far more justice and depth to an account of the customs and etiquette of Ghana than a foreign guidebook could ever do.

Home visits

To appreciate the real Ghanaian experience, seek out one of the many tour operators who place you, at least for a part of your visit, with a host family. The family will be delighted to have you (if you behave appropriately) and you will be equally delighted to be in the midst of a lovely family who can teach you much about Ghanaian life, customs, and etiquette.

Cultural Tours

Tour operators who offer a real cultural experience, rather than simply a hotel room and taxi to the airport, are listed on page 165.

SPORTS AND GAMES

Football (soccer) is definitely the king of sports in Ghana. The country went wild during 2006 when the Black Stars made their first World Cup appearance and went on to become the only African nation to make it out of the group stages. The streets were once again blocked by singing and dancing fans during CAN 2008, hosted by Ghana, which achieved a formidable

third place. The two big club teams are Hearts of Oak from Accra and Asante Kotoko from Kumasi. Visitors who express a slight interest in football may be immediately asked if they are "Phobia" (Hearts supporter) or "Fabulous" (Kotoko supporter). Foreign football, especially the English league, is extremely popular, and many television centers' blackboards bear something like "Manchester United v Liverpool, 8 p.m." Boxing, table tennis, track-and-field, and volleyball are other favorites.

Some of the time spent sitting under trees and on wooden benches is also filled with playing board games. Ludo and draughts (*dami*) are very popular imports. Cards are played, but there seems to be only one known card game, called "Spar." This consists of throwing away all the 2s, 3s, 4s, and 5s before seeing who can slam the remaining cards down hardest on the table. The most common local game is Oware, an ancient game similar to backgammon, which you should have a go at. Hand-carved Oware sets make great presents to take back home.

HIKING

Ghanaians do not understand the idea of walking for pleasure. Unless you are a farmer, logger, hunter, or mineral prospector, you should have no business in the forest. Ecotourism is on the increase, however, and there are plenty of great walks offering panoramic views, interesting nature, and insights into traditional ways of life.

Walking in "the bush" is also a great way to meet people and learn about ways of life that you never see when traveling on the roads. If you strike up a conversation with a pawpaw, cocoa, orange, pineapple, or banana farmer, then he's sure to offer you some of his fresh  produce. If you don't meet anybody, however, helping yourself is discouraged.

Visitors should not come to Ghana expecting to see the "big game" that is more common throughout eastern and southern Africa, although there are elephants, crocodiles, and some very elusive chimpanzees. The smaller birds, butterflies, bats, driver ants, monkeys, mammals, reptiles, and multitudinous tree and plant species are sufficient, though, for a great nature experience. The mountains, forests, waterfalls, and rivers also offer some wonderfully secluded spots for meditation. The enchanted hills around the town of Kibi are a hiker's dream.

LITERATURE

A lifetime is not long enough for an avid reader in Balme Library at the University of Ghana, Legon. Entry is free, and you can sit for hours reading some very old books about Ghanaian and Gold Coast history. The 1920s British colonial teacher and historian W. E. F. Ward offers some engrossing insights into the history and culture of the Gold Coast at that time.

Excellent Ghanaian authors abound, and interested readers should look out for Ayi Kwei Armah, Efua Sutherland, Kofi Awoonor, and Ama Ata Aiddo. The most famous stories are the folktales about the cunning but greedy spiderman, Kwaku Ananse. The most comprehensive collection of African and international literature, music, and movies is available at Silverbird in Accra Mall.

Orally, humorous anecdotes known as "Toli" are often told, as are jokes about the negative traits of Ghanaians.

Ghana Hell

More self-deprecating humor:

A man dies and goes to hell. Once there, he finds that there is a different hell for each country and he çan choose which one he prefers. He asks what happens in Germany hell, and is told: "First you are put in the electric chair for an hour, then they lay you on a bed of nails for an hour, then the German devil whips you for the rest of the day." Not fancying that, he asks about the American, Chinese, British, and French hells and finds out that they all offer the same treatment. He then notices a long line of people waiting to get into the Ghana hell and asks what happens in there. He is told: "First you are put in the electric chair for an hour, then they lay you on a bed of nails for an hour, then the Ghanaian devil whips you for the rest of the day."

"But that's the same as all the others," he says. "Why are so many people waiting to get in?"

"Because there is never any electricity, so the electric chair doesn't work. The nails were paid for, but never supplied, so the bed is comfortable. And, on top of it all, the Ghanaian devil used to be a civil servant, so he just comes in, signs his time sheet, then goes back out on private business for the rest of the day."

TRAVEL, HEALTH, & SAFETY

Ghana's road system is a mixed bag. Many new, good-quality roads and expressways offer the visitor some comfortable and memorable coastal, mountain, or forest drives. Tourists wanting to explore Ghana in their own or public transportation should have few, if any, problems, and the journeys are often as entertaining as the destination. Ghanaians will go out of their way to help a lost stranger, and vehicle crime is extremely uncommon. People are friendly and sociable on transport, but conversation is limited by noise and Ghanaians' lack of small talk. Foreigners who feel the urge to fill a journey with a hundred needless questions are teasingly referred to as "What's the name of that bird?" tourists.

On the other hand, some roads can be of very inferior quality, some vehicles are not roadworthy, accidents are common, traffic is often a nightmare, and driving etiquette leaves a lot to be desired. These risks can be considerably lessened by using a little common sense, and traveling on Ghana's roads remains a favorite tourist attraction, if not for the fainthearted.

ROADS AND TRAFFIC

Take a journey along the coast from Accra to
Winneba, or through the mountains to Aburi, to
witness just two examples of well-built new roads
in Ghana. New road building is a government
priority. However, many tarmac roads soon lose
their integrity, with potholes in the middle or
increasingly big "bites" being taken from the sides.
Regular drivers usually know all the potholes on
their routes by heart. Road repairs are not
undertaken hastily, and can often be no more
than a sand infill. "Bush" roads can have huge
crevasses ripped into them from the rains, or just
turn to quicksand during the rainy season. People
are rushing to snap up land to build their houses,
without the roads to get to them. Access even
to some big hotels, housing estates, and luxurious
private homes involves some pretty tricky
driving conditions.

Vehicles

Vehicles are often not
roadworthy or overloaded,
but a gift to the policeman is
all it takes to solve this
problem. Unfortunately this
allows vehicles that are not
roadworthy to stay on the
road. Ghanaian drivers
generally do not follow the
rules of the road, nor are
they required to have any

driving lessons before getting their license. Some drivers feel the need for "Dutch courage" before taking to the roads, and speeding is just another way of getting more fares in one day. It is illegal to drive when drunk or to have a dilapidated vehicle, but these rules are never enforced. As a result, traffic accidents are common. Drivers never obey lane rules—if there is a space, a car will fill it. A driver coming onto a main road will demand to be let in rather than waiting for an invitation.

For those with the means, car rental firms abound and are advertised in all the tourist brochures. If you are staying in a good hotel, it's usually best to arrange your car rental from there. It is also advisable to hire a driver, too, in order to avoid getting lost, stranded, or completely baffled by the road rules. Four-wheel-drive vehicles are useful, even in the streets of the capital.

Addresses

Maps of Ghana and the cities are readily available, but addresses can be hard to find. Addresses are listed by post office box numbers, which could be in a different area from the person's residence. Roads do not generally have names or numbers, although the larger roads and newer housing estates may do so. The signboards of businesses usually give you the best idea of which area you're in. To meet someone at their home or business for the first time might require instructions such as: "Take a car to Roundabout. Tell the driver you will get down at Curve. Walk down to the Spot. After the Filling Station. Opposite the Chop Bar.

Ask for Maame Ataa the banana seller. Call me
and I'll meet you there."

Driving

If you are driving by yourself, be aware of the
following. Ghana drives on the right. You will need
an international driver's permit and your vehicle
should have the necessary tax, insurance, Ministry
of Transport test
certificate, hazard
triangle, and fire
extinguisher. A car
flashing its headlights
at you is demanding
the right of way, not
allowing you the right
of way. Horns are used
regularly, to mean "Hello," "Where are you going?,"
"Get out of my way," "I have empty seats," or to get
the goats out of the street. Piles of leaves or grass
in the road, or sometimes someone waving leaves,
mean "Slow down" for an accident or blockage.
Police barriers can stop you at fixed or random
locations to check your vehicle and
documentation. Make sure everything is in order
or they will make things difficult for you. A
policeman moving his torch up and down means
"stop," and left to right means "go."

As Ghanaians are becoming wealthier, one of
their most treasured items, often before a house, is
a car. More and more people own their own
vehicles, either imported by Ghanaians abroad,
bought from the many salesmen in Ghana, or

driven in across the borders. Public transportation also abounds. Certainly in Accra one can get the impression that there are far too many taxis. Too many cars and not enough roads, unintelligent traffic light systems, police barriers, accidents, street parades, construction, and herds of animals can all contribute to some critically bad traffic congestion in the cities. Traffic is a common excuse for Ghanaians' lateness, most of the time a justifiable one. Motorbikes and bicycles are good traffic dodgers, but less safe. It is a legal requirement to wear a motorcycle helmet, but this law is commonly flouted. In fact, try to avoid the rush hours. Traveling on a Sunday morning in eerily deserted streets can be bliss.

You can buy virtually anything from the comfort of your car. Many areas or towns also have their specialties displayed on the roadside, such as a town

of a thousand bread sellers or a road dominated by palm oil or *gari* (grated cassava) stands. On the village roads there are fruit and vegetable stands, along with small children offering up such delicacies as snails, crabs, mushrooms, rat, and the delicious grasscutter (cane rat).

Walking

Walking in Ghana's streets is a uniquely entertaining experience. As long as you take care where you're putting your feet and don't mind the sun, the crowds, the slow pace of other pedestrians, the constant beeping of taxi horns, the confusing directions, and the only measure of distance given being "far" or "not far," then walking can give you a glimpse into Ghanaian life that isn't noticed from a vehicle. It also gives you the opportunity to make more friends.

The roads and sidewalks can be a real risk to unwary pedestrians, however. "Hit by a car" is an all too common cause for grief. Be very careful when crossing roads, especially at night, as lights on cars and bikes do not always shine. Town pavements are flanked by deep rain gutters that are almost invariably uncovered. Even the covered gutters will have random slabs missing, ready to trap those who drop their guard. In most areas, the gutters do a decent job of channeling the deluges of the rainy season. In addition, they offer a never-ending source of raw material for anyone wanting to invest in plastic recycling.

Flip-flops, the tourists' perennial favorite footwear, are known locally as *chale wote* (pronounced "Charlie Wotty"), meaning, "My friend, let's go" in Ga. They can be quickly slipped on when your friend beckons you to come out. It's probably true to say that every Ghanaian who can walk owns a pair of *chale wote*. A Ghanaian will give them the English name of "bathroom slippers," and they are mainly used for going and coming to the bathroom, or just around the house. Many people do, however, wear them outside. For some it may be all they can afford. It's much easier for a Muslim in *chale wote* to perform his ablutions before prayers, or for a visitor to remove them when entering a house. There are three reasons, however, for visitors to reconsider their use of *chale wote*. Firstly, white-skinned visitors will quickly develop an unsightly ankle-deep layer of Ghana's ubiquitous red dust, with a possible extra layer of muddy puddle or animal deposit. Many areas will be rough road with plenty of loose stones and potholes ready to break your toes and sprain your ankles. Finally, and most importantly, etiquette demands that when working or traveling, one should dress smartly. This includes nice shoes.

PUBLIC TRANSPORTATION

In terms of availability, cost, patronage, and coverage area, Ghana's public transportation system is excellent. Visitors are often impressed by how easily and cheaply they can get around the country. Walking into a station or waiting at a bus stop for the first time can be a bewildering experience, but once you understand the system and know where to get the cars you want, it's very straightforward. Depending upon your budget, there are three main modes of transport.

Dropping Taxis

Taxis are easily identifiable by their orange or yellow painted corners. One travel writer recently stated he would not be surprised to hear that 80 percent of the vehicles on Ghana's roads were

taxis. They come in various stages of upkeep, but the drivers are always approachable and extremely keen for your business. "Dropping" means taking you where you want to go with no other passengers. The fare should be agreed to first, so make sure you know how much your journey would cost a Ghanaian, to avoid being overcharged. Gasoline costs have risen highly over the past few years, so don't barter too hard or be too stingy. If he's a good driver, give him a tip or buy him something from the hawkers. Taxis can also be hired by the day. Most Ghanaians only take dropping taxis occasionally, or only for short distances, as the price is more than ten times that of shared transport. Even for tourists, taking dropping everywhere is a surefire way to see your dollars quickly disappear.

Shared Taxis
Shared taxis ply certain routes for a fixed fare. Their destinations are identified by either a sign

on the roof, the driver shouting, or by asking anyone in the station. They leave when their four seats are full, but customers may pay for a last remaining seat if they are in a hurry. People generally greet each other when getting into a shared taxi, but usually not when getting into a tro-tro.

Tro-tros

Ask anyone who has visited Ghana to recount some memorable experiences from their vacation, and among the tales of the beautiful beaches, exciting nightlife, and wonderful people will always be found several tro-tro anecdotes. Riding on these various forms of minibus is a popular tourist attraction, and the commonest and cheapest mode of transport for Ghanaians. Some can be dirty, crowded, and falling apart, and are appropriately called "boneshakers," but they can still get you from one side of Accra to another for less than a dollar and are a great way to observe the people and environment.

Tro-tros have three seats accessible from the front door (including the driver's), with the remaining seats at the back reached through a sliding door on the side. Many doors require a special technique to open, and are held on by ropes.

Tro-tros have a driver and a mate (conductor). They can be found at stations or stopped anywhere along their route. The route will be shouted out by the mate, who also takes your money. Extra seats are

THE TRO-TRO UNIVERSE

Traveling in tro-tros has gained such a cult following among visitors that over 1,000 people have joined the "Tro-tro appreciation society" on www.facebook.com, which contains the following humorous observations:

Time does not exist in the tro-tro universe. It will leave when it's full, and will get there sometime after that.

The optimum temperature for the inside of a tro-tro should exceed that of the core of the sun, so all passengers can sweat freely on their neighbors.

A person occupies a seat. If you have luggage as big as a person, you must still wedge it on your knees until your toes turn blue. Goats must be tied to the roof.

In the event of a crash, under no circumstances should a tro-tro pull over: it must remain in the middle of the road until the drivers have finished fighting.

A speedometer is an unnecessary distraction. The speed settings are "regular," "fast," and "crashed."

In order to optimize the "experience" of Ghana's roads, no tro-tro should employ suspension of any kind.

A gear stick should have anything but a gear knob on it, for example a tap or a golf ball.

A tro-tro is made up of 40 percent seat, 10 percent wheels, 20 percent (and falling) floor, ceiling, and sides, and 30 percent rope/gaffer tape.

usually welded into the aisle of a tro-tro, and are folded up to let passengers get to the back. Getting in and out of tro-tros can be quite a chore—don't go to sit at the back if you know you're getting out soon. It's better to sit in the window seats on the left: no getting up to let people out, you get the breeze and easy access to the hawkers, and have an escape route in the event of a crash. The best seat is generally considered to be the front passenger seat by the window. There are two passenger seats at the front, with the one immediately to the right of the driver being the most uncomfortable. Somebody who has bagged the window seat will get out when someone else comes in, letting the newcomer onto the uncomfortable seat.

Riding on tro-tros, like the rest of life in Ghana, is communal. Be prepared to carry other people's luggage and children on and off, pass money from the backseat, and join in with the other passengers shouting at the driver to slow down or stop passing recklessly.

Relatively recent additions to Ghana's roads are the big yellow coaches known as "Kufuor Buses," which are technically giant tro-tros.

A ferry service is available along the Volta Lake.

Inscriptions

Many a tourist's favorite pastime in Ghana is reading the wonderful slogans and other inscriptions that drivers put on the back of their vehicles. Many have religious connotations, such as "Christ is my Redeemer," "Who Jah Bless, No Man Curse," and "God is my Seatbelt." Others are sayings such as "No Food for Lazy Man," "Life is War," "Police is your Friend," and "My Best Friend is my Ten Fingers." Others can defy explanation, like "Bomboclat Buffalo!" "Observers are Worried," and "No Shaking."

Proud drivers will often add "Still . . ." to the beginning of their vehicles' names after an unspecified period of having managed to survive Ghana's roads without crashing or blowing up.

Inscriptions in the vernacular are widespread and offer great practice for language learners, such as the following examples in Twi:

Enye mahooden: It is not my strength (that helps me; it is God's).

Onipa nfon kwa: People do not get thin for no reason.

Asem da onipa so atemuda: Judgment Day awaits us.

INTERCITY TRAVEL
Planes
The modern and well-serviced Kotoka International Airport handles more than 170 weekly flights to more than thirty-six destinations. Domestic flights can also be taken to Kumasi and Tamale.

Trains
The train lines from Accra to Kumasi to Sekondi to Accra form a triangle that was originally designed for the quick extraction of raw materials rather than the transport of people. They can, however, be an interesting mode of transportation and another good way to meet the locals.

STCs
These large, air-conditioned, safe coaches from the State Transport Company are the best choice for intercity travel. They generally leave on time. It is a good idea to buy your ticket beforehand.

WHERE TO STAY
Hotels
Ghana has a wide selection of hotels and guesthouses to suit every visitor. The exclusive La Palm Hotel, complete with casino, world-class restaurant, five-star accommodation, and international price range, is one of the hotels of choice for visiting oil tycoons and American presidents. On the other hand, those on a budget can get a decent room in a guesthouse for US $10.

Renting

Rooms or houses for rent are also plentiful, as are the agents and their signboards advertising them. The rent is usually payable up front, for a minimum of one or two years, but it works out much cheaper than paying for a hotel for the same period.

HEALTH

All visitors to Ghana should seek and act on proper medical advice from their doctor at least two months prior to departure, and look on the Internet for up-to-date travel advice. There are, however, some general tips that can be given.

Precautions

To be prepared, bring the following items with you: prescription medicines, plasters, bandages, antiseptic, rehydration salts, sunblock, syringes, water sterilization tablets, daily vitamins, and blood group card.

The only inoculation certificate required for entry to Ghana is that for yellow fever. One shot will last for ten years. Your doctor will also prescribe shots for rabies, meningitis, polio, typhoid, diphtheria, and hepatitis. Africa's biggest killer, malaria, is present in Ghana, and the usual precautions and prophylactic drugs should be taken. Oral prophylaxis drugs such as chloroquine, paludrine or larium should be discussed with your doctor. The course should be taken from at least two weeks before you arrive until four weeks after you return, but you will be able to buy extra supplies from main drugstores in Ghana. Of course, if you don't get bitten by mosquitoes, you won't get malaria.

Even if these stave off malaria, mosquitoes can still give an itchy and unsightly bite. Avoid living in areas close to standing water where mosquito larvae breed. Use a mosquito net, insecticide, and a repellent containing deet. Cover up exposed skin as much as possible after dusk. Feet and ankles seem to be a prime site for bites, so mosquitoes love visitors who wear sandals and flip-flops. The most common defense used by Ghanaians is the relatively cheap mosquito coil, a kind of antimosquito incense. Try to keep babies and young children inside after dusk. For fair-skinned visitors, protection from the sun with a hat and/or high factor sunscreen is a must.

Note that sunscreen is not widely available in Ghana.

Apart from the mosquitoes, there are lots of other nasties and creepy-crawlies that will want to bite you, poison you, live inside you, crawl over your face when you're sleeping, latch onto you when you're swimming, and share your house. It's not advisable to pet unknown dogs or cats in case of rabies. Be prepared for extra houseguests in the form of lizards, mice, cockroaches, and various ants. In some areas, the sky can be filled at certain times with clouds of flying ants whose bodies will carpet your floor underneath any attractive light. Most of these beasts are annoying but harmless.

It's up to you how strictly you follow your doctor's advice about these creatures. To be ultracautious, don't walk in the forest in case of snakes, and don't bathe in the rivers in case of river blindness.

Food and Water

Another useful drug to pack is a fast-acting antidiarrheal remedy. Diarrhea is common for first-time visitors, but it never lasts long and some degree of immunity is often built up after the first attack. Check the food and water you are consuming.

Water in Ghana comes in several forms. Medical advice is that untreated water be filtered and boiled before use. It was only earlier this decade that the selling of "ice water" on the streets was banned. This was chilled water from unknown sources sold in plastic bags. Sometimes you could still see the algae and floating bits from the river it was taken from. Street sellers offer "pure water," which is licensed, filtered water sold in printed plastic bags. Some fussy visitors are even scared of this, and go for the more expensive mineral water sold in bottles. Many communities have an open well or river for water, but these are mainly used for washing rather than drinking. Boreholes are also common, drawing from the water table some meters under the bedrock. This is more drinkable than well water, and also comes out nicely chilled. Many houses have pipe-borne water, but it is uncommon to see people drinking this. Some medical advice even warns against brushing your teeth with it. All sorts of soft drinks, beers, fruit juices, milks, and other beverages are common and safe.

Choosing food to eat in Ghana has been described as both a nightmare for fussy eaters and a paradise for more open-minded visitors who are ready to learn about a whole new cuisine. It makes for a much richer experience to try as much new food as you can, but, again, there are some general guidelines. Despite the health benefits of salad and the wide array of fresh ingredients available, it is still recommended by some that travelers avoid salads and peeled fruit, as they may have been prepared in unhygienic conditions. You can always make it yourself at home. If buying cooked food on the streets, look at the general state of the place and the people selling the food. Try not to buy anything that has been cooked some time ago and left open to the flies, being sold next to the stinky gutter by the vendor with dirty hands. To be safe, always ask for something straight from the frying pan or oven, not from the display cabinet.

Most food is eaten with the fingers, so wash hands thoroughly first. For Ghanaians, the maxim "The left hand washes the right, and the right hand washes the left" seems to be used only metaphorically, and a quick dip of the right hand into a communal washing bowl with no soap is the norm. Soap and running water will be provided on request, and will often come in the form of a friend pouring a jug of water for you.

Toilets

A common Ghanaian practice that foreigners usually do not like to adopt is the storage of used toilet paper in a box in the bathroom, burning it rather than flushing it away. It might "block the system," and certainly leads to a quicker filling of the cesspits that most toilets empty into. This requires the costly services of the "Suck Away" truck to empty. You can find a decent flush toilet to use in most places, even if the flush is from pouring down a bucket of water. The public toilets usually don't flush, are pretty dirty, and give you only newspaper, not toilet paper. In more disadvantaged areas, the toilet will be a wooden seat over a bucket. There is a small "back door" for the bucket emptiers to do their dirty work. Still common in remote villages is the toilet facility with the delightful onomatopoeic name sounding like "Schweeee—tum," describing a large hole crisscrossed with planks, over which you crouch.

Despite "Do not urinate here" signs on walls all over the towns, Ghanaians (including women) freely urinate outside (or in a "public toilet" that leads straight into the gutter). Just watch where you're stepping and check that the place you're buying your food doesn't also double as a urinal. Public toilets seem to go against the general expectations of personal hygiene, often even with nowhere to wash your hands. The tourist board goes so far as to recommend visitors use the facilities in hotels or restaurants, because of the low sanitation standards in public facilities.

A wake-up call to Ghana came with the publication of a 2008 report by UNICEF and the World Health Organization ranking Ghana a shocking forty-eighth out of fifty-one countries in Africa for levels of sanitation.

HIV/AIDS

Although Ghana has a lower infection rate than many other African countries, it remains a serious and real problem. International and local funding are largely directed toward prevention and treatment of HIV/AIDS. The British volunteer agency VSO requires *all* its recruits, even if they are working as a fish farmer or an accountant, to work toward at least one HIV/AIDS-related objective. The government's "Stop Aids, Love Life" campaign with its messages of abstinence, fidelity, and "If it's not on, it's not in" has also helped to raise the profile of HIV/AIDS. However, despite widespread knowledge of STDs, people continue to become infected. Some Ghanaian men will freely admit that they prefer to do it "raw," and that they can find women to participate in unsafe sex with them for a fee. Tourists are advised that the infection rate of STDs in Ghana is high, and should always use condoms (which are widely available) if entering into sexual relationships.

Medical Treatment

If you require medical treatment, you will find no lack of facilities in Ghana, except in the isolated villages. Ghana has a modern medical system funded and administered by the government, with some participation from church groups, international agencies, and NGOs. Privately owned drugstores also sell a wide range of medicines over the counter. Drugstore workers can usually give you the correct prescription if you describe your symptoms, but they are not trained medical staff. Medical insurance is of course advised, but be aware that medical providers may not accept payment through your insurance company, leaving you to pay first, then file a reimbursement claim later. Or, for a real cultural experience, would you be prepared to pay a visit to the witch doctor?

SAFETY

Ghana is a very safe country, and its proud, peace-loving inhabitants are determined to keep it so. A lone female can walk the streets of Ghana at midnight with a wallet full of dollars without a worry, and the only form of violence you will see is the "mob justice" handed out by loyal citizens when a thief is caught red-handed, or occasionally when a driver knocks someone down. If anyone is being harassed or threatened, passing strangers will jump to their aid immediately.

However, crime is not unknown in Ghana, and tourists can be a prime target. Again, use your common sense and follow some simple guidelines. The most dangerous areas (mainly from pickpockets and opportunistic thieves) are inevitably the tourist areas, such as the airport, Osu in Accra, and the popular beaches, especially at night. Don't flash your money around and keep most of it in a safe place, taking just what you need for the day in your wallet or pocket. Change foreign currency in the designated places, not with the guys in the street. Some cases have been reported of shared taxis being used for armed robberies at night. Walk with a friend if you feel unsafe.

419

"419" is the name given to e-mail scams, originally from Nigeria, although the practice is growing in Ghana, where it has become known as *sakawa*. Some "*sakawa* boys" are known to perform juju rituals before logging on to increase their chances of success. If contacting Ghana over the Internet, do not entertain anyone telling you they have millions of dollars in a foreign account that could be yours if you help them to release it, or who claim to have gold and diamonds for sale. Also be very careful if using any of the plethora of dating sites, as not all potential partners are what they purport to be. Some Internet cafés are full of unscrupulous men using the lure of a beautiful young woman to attract foreigners looking for dates. Many cafés are now putting up "No 419 activities here" signs.

Sexual Harassment

Western women can often become fed up with, or sometimes feel intimidated by, constant advances from the sexually liberated Ghana Man, who can be quite unabashed in his quest for a white woman, and will commonly approach strangers in the street to declare his love. Most approaches are in jest, and can be answered in a similar fashion. Try something like "Oh really! You're the tenth husband I've got today!" or "My husband is just on his way—you'll have to ask him." Or "I can't marry a Ghanaian—I don't know how to cook fufu!" It has been said that fake wedding rings work very well too. If you do feel at all unsafe, just call for a passing stranger to get rid of pesky men for you. And don't get into a situation where there's no passing stranger to help you. Similar offers to men are also commonplace, and also usually in jest. You'll lose count of the number of sisters, daughters, granddaughters, and sometimes even wives who are offered to you to marry and take back to your country. Be aware that inviting a member of the opposite sex into your bedroom will be seen as an invitation for sex.

Accidents

Road accidents and drowning are the two most common causes of tourist death. STCs are the safest transport, and you should avoid traveling at night. If you don't trust the vehicle or the driver, get another one.

The sea current is very dangerous. Popular beaches have patrolled zones with lifeguards in canoes.

Don't make the all-too-common mistake of stretching or taking off your shirt while standing under a low ceiling fan.

When enjoying a walk in the forest, don't hold or lean against the trees and branches with spikes and poisonous ants on them. Wear high boots to protect against snakebite, and bash the bush ahead of you with a stick to scare snakes away.

THE ENVIRONMENT

Ghana's peaceful towns, lush forests, and beautiful beaches are rapidly being covered in rubbish, especially plastic waste. Recycling and proper disposal of waste has yet to catch on, and no visitor will leave Ghana without witnessing the unsightly and unhygienic rubbish dumps all over the country. It is common to see people dropping litter on the ground in the knowledge that someone will probably sweep it up later. Even in the capital, trash cans are hard to find, and, wherever you are in the country, you'll probably see a pure water sachet on the floor. In addition, toilet facilities are not accessible to all, and some areas, notably the beaches in Accra, can be disgusting areas to walk on.

The most noticeable sign of the government's fight against rubbish is the bicycle army called "Zoom Lion," contracted street cleaners who are employed to sweep up all the rubbish from an area and dump it somewhere else. Companies producing plastic products are being asked to make a contribution to the cost of dealing with their waste. Visitors can do their bit by using fewer plastic bags, or making protection of the environment one of their key criteria for investing in businesses.

The other example of environmental degradation that has many a sympathetic visitor in tears is deforestation. The timber industry and the clearing of land for farms and buildings have taken an awful toll on the once mighty rain forests. It is possible to see loggers in action across the country. The time to do something to combat this, for local and worldwide reasons, is now. Ecotourism and proper management of the timber industry have the biggest potential to save the Ghanaian forests.

chapter eight

BUSINESS BRIEFING

Ghana is internationally renowned as a safe place for investment and business with high human resource levels. The numbers of expatriate workers in Ghana are mushrooming. The discovery in 2007 of large reserves of oil will no doubt bring many more. Several high-profile companies have relocated to Ghana owing to the instability in some surrounding West African countries. Numbers of volunteers and aid workers are also high. Ghana strives to meet the needs of these multifarious visitors, and usually succeeds. It is justifiably known as Africa's Golden Gateway for Investment, and is on course to realize its goal of achieving middle-income status by 2020.

It is also a place where things can move slowly in business, and there is no shortage of frustrations for foreign workers. Bribes or gifts (depending upon your outlook) are commonplace in order to speed up processes, land a contract, etc. Fraud and reneging on agreements are not unknown. There are plenty of honest, hardworking, skilled employees or business partners, but also others who lack such integrity.

INVESTING

The government encourages investment in the following growth areas: cotton and textiles; ethnic beauty products; financial services; transport services; property development; ceramics; apparel; agro-processing; cash crops; seafood processing; furniture and wood processing; information technology and electronics; floriculture; fine and custom jewelry; tourism; construction; real estate; waste recycling.

Anyone planning to invest in Ghana should first contact the Ghana Investment Promotion Center (GIPC). The GIPC was established under the Ghana Investment Promotion Center Act of 1994 to provide economic, commercial, and investment information for entrepreneurs interested in starting a business or investing in Ghana. The GIPC is a government agency with two primary objectives: the encouragement and promotion of investment in the Ghanaian economy, and the coordination and monitoring of all investment activities.

Prior to establishing a business entity in Ghana, it is advisable to consult a local lawyer. Details of recommended lawyers are provided by the Commercial Service. Lawyers may also be required for managing disagreements and making sure that contracts are followed through as agreed to, or advising on business law. In dealing with disputes, a quiet word on the side will be much more productive than criticizing someone publicly.

FACILITIES

Business facilities, especially in the big cities, are very good. Accra International Conference Centre can hold over one thousand people. Hotels, car rentals, international phone calls, Internet access, faxing, printing, air mail, door-to-door delivery services, conference rooms, satellite TV, and so on are all easy to come by and mainly cheap (an hour in an Internet café still costs less than a dollar).

Business hours vary. Accra is a twenty-four-hour city in many places, but the usual business hours are 8:00 a.m. to 5:00 p.m., Monday to Saturday, sometimes with a lunch break. Banks are usually open from 8:30 a.m. to 3:00 p.m., although some may close earlier. Allow plenty of time for a visit to the bank. Big banks have twenty-four-hour ATM machines with armed guards, but there is a cash limit on these machines. Don't expect to get much business done on a Sunday.

MONEY

There is no limit on the amount of foreign currency you may bring into Ghana, although taking money out of the country is subject to restrictions. Most easily used are dollars, pounds, or Euros, which can be changed at banks, hotels, and the ubiquitous forex bureaux, or indeed used for purchases without changing into local currency. To be safer from loss or theft, major credit cards and traveler's checks can also be used. However, credit cards have been known to be used for fraud, and traveler's checks are less easily changed than cash.

The national currency up to July 2007 was the cedi. High inflation (15 percent in 2005) meant that thousands, millions, and even billions of cedis were being used and quoted in everyday life. This led to the redenomination of the currency into the Ghana cedi, with 10,000 old cedis being replaced by one Ghana cedi, divided into 100 Ghana 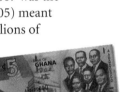 pesewas. One Ghana cedi is currently just less than one US dollar. After six confusing months of both currencies being used together, the Ghana cedi became the sole official currency in January 2008. For many people, this change is proving hard to get used to, and it is now common to see purchases made in the new money while the prices quoted are in the old. A first-time visitor will have to get used to ten Ghana cedis being referred to as a hundred thousand, one hundred as one million, and ten pesewas as a thousand.

There always seems to be a shortage of change in Ghana. Try to buy a packet of chewing gum with a 50-Ghana-cedi note, and you will not receive a favorable reaction. Some people even make a living by selling coins. If you have the correct change, especially for rides, this will make life a lot easier.

WORK IN GHANA

Even with the business boom, Ghana remains a predominantly rural, agro- and mineral exporting nation with 60 percent of the working population engaged in agriculture. The adult unemployment rate is officially 9 percent. An afternoon's drive through parts of any town might give you the impression that everybody in Ghana is employed

in selling foreign goods from small wooden shops or metal containers. Every morning, they bring out their displays of cookies, tires, fridges, soft drinks, suitcases, etc., etc., only to load it all back in again in the evening, complaining that there is "no market." The names of some of these smaller businesses can be just as entertaining as the taxi and tro-tro inscriptions, as is the apparent desire to come up with the catchiest possible acronym for a business or professional group.

Ghanaians are beginning to realize that there's more money to be made in manufacturing goods in their own country than from exporting raw materials. However, industrial production comprises only 10 percent of national output.

Many businesspeople are involved in politics, have lived abroad, or have "bogga" relations who are able to send them money or foreign goods to set up a business. The Lebanese and Asian (primarily Indian) communities play an important role in business in Ghana. Many Lebanese businesspeople are third- and fourth-generation Ghanaian citizens. This group dominates much of the import of dry goods, furniture and fixtures, building materials, and durable goods.

"Ghana Man Time"

If you are doing business or working with Ghanaians, you will be happy to find a smartly dressed, articulate, polite, and skilled workforce. You will also unfortunately encounter your fair share of procrastination and lax attitude toward appointments. Expect meetings to be late, cancelled, or forgotten. Ghanaians themselves bemoan their own unpunctuality and jokingly refer to their own version of GMT: "Ghana Man" or "Ghana Maybe" Time. To help pass some of the time you will spend sitting in tro-tros and plastic chairs, just look around and count how many people are wearing broken watches. A recent government campaign addressing the problem carried the message: "I am proud to be a Ghanaian—be punctual to work and appointments!" Traffic congestion is a commonly used and often justifiable excuse.

Customer service is also very poor in many businesses, and even within the government. Female secretaries, cashiers, and sales assistants are frequently very good at giving you the impression that by entering their premises you are disturbing them while they are dozing, calling their boyfriends on their mobile phones, or eating their *kenkey*. Orderly lines at busy shops and bus stops do not exist.

Meetings

Business in Ghana is very Westernized, although traditional values also extend to business dealings. Politeness, greetings, and handshakes with all present are expected. Ghanaians like regular, face-to-face contact and personal visits are warmly welcomed. While paying personal visits may not always be the most efficient or inexpensive method, it is generally regarded as the most effective method for handling business initiatives.

In order to make contact with businesses and develop a relationship, you should actively pursue them; don't wait around for promised phone calls. Make sure your initial introduction is polite and, if the contact is in person, that you are smartly dressed. People in senior positions in business and public institutions expect their juniors and guests to accord them due respect and to address them correctly. This is also true for foreign guests. A letter detailing your proposals should be handed over at your first meeting, or possibly sent in advance in order to get a first meeting. Follow up with phone calls.

Dealing with secretaries can be very frustrating —it's best to deal with the top man (or, nowadays, increasingly, top woman) if you can. Having a trusted local link is very beneficial. It's not what you know, it's who you know.

> **Local Contacts: A Proviso**
> *Many foreigners wishing to invest in businesses, or Ghanaians abroad sending money back to Ghana for the building of a home, rely on a local contact to receive this money and ensure that it is used for the purpose intended. In many cases, however, these people arrive in Ghana expecting to see the work in progress, only to realize that their contact has pocketed it all. It is of vital importance to find somebody you can really trust for these transactions.*

If you are importing goods into Ghana, you will find an awful lot of red tape, delays, and hidden taxes. Companies now offer international door-to-door shipping, which is much better than several unproductive trips to Tema port to clear your own goods.

Business cards are widely used in Ghana, so be sure to have an adequate supply. It is common practice to give a business card to almost everyone you meet in a business setting, so bring plenty.

If you are holding a meeting with someone, it is useful to phone more than once to make sure it is still on, and make sure everybody knows when and where to meet. If attending a training course, workshop, or conference, Ghanaians will first want to ensure that their transport costs are provided and that suitable refreshments are available. Otherwise expect very little participation. Interruptions during meetings are common. Mobile phones regularly go off even during parliamentary meetings and live newscasts.

The business hierarchy is very "top-down" and an initial meeting with the director or executive officer is recommended. Once he or she gives the green light to the underlings to work with you, then they will give you all the help you require.

Once the pleasantries of greetings are over with, you will expected to get straight to the point and be factual, not waste time on flowery presentations. You will be listened to carefully and questioned at length. The main (or sole) point of discussions will be money—everybody will want to know how much you are offering, then try to increase this, so expect bargaining to take place.

Bribery

Bribery, or asking for "favors," may well be encountered in business circles, even if it is not directly requested. Depending on your views, this will be seen either as a natural extension of gift giving, or downright corruption. The unfortunate fact remains that contracts can be awarded, jobs offered, or proposals accepted not on merit, but on the size of the bribe. Visitors will see open bribery at roadblocks of police, who need to augment their meager incomes somehow.

The Contractor

This is a joke Ghanaians tell about themselves.

Three contractors were visiting a tourist attraction on the same day. One was from Ghana, the other from Germany, and the third from the USA. At the end of the tour, the guide asked them what they did for a living. When they all replied that they were contractors, the guide said, "Hey, we need one of the rear fences redone. Why don't you guys take a look at it and give me a bid?" So, to the back fence they all went to check it out.

First to step up was the German contractor. He took out his tape measure and pencil, did some measuring and said, "Well, I figure the job will run to about nine hundred dollars: four hundred for materials, four hundred for my crew, and a hundred profit for me."

Next was the American contractor. He also took out his tape measure and pencil, did some quick figuring and said, "Looks like I can do this job for seven hundred dollars: three hundred for materials, three hundred for my crew, and a hundred profit for me."

Without so much as moving, the Ghanaian contractor said, "Two thousand seven hundred." The guide, incredulous, looked at him and said, "You didn't even measure like the other guys! How did you come up with such a high figure?"

"Easy," he said, pulling the guide to one side and lowering his voice. "A thousand for you, a thousand for me, and we hire the guy from America."

Corruption in Ghana is less of a problem than in other countries in the region, but companies cannot expect complete transparency in locally funded contracts. The 2004 Transparency International global corruption ranking placed Ghana 64th out of 146 countries in its Corruption Perceptions Index, and the seventh-least corrupt country in Africa. Ghana gets a "moderate" rating in the Public Integrity Index, which tracks a country's levels of corruption, openness, and accountability.

President Kufuor has declared "zero tolerance" of corruption. He has established an Office of Accountability to oversee the performance of senior government functionaries. Several corruption prosecutions are under way against former officials of the Rawlings administration, and a former minister is now in jail. Two other ministers are also in jail for their role in causing financial loss to the state.

DEALING WITH THE GOVERNMENT

As with all business culture in the country, trying to work with the Ghanaian government can be frustrating and time-consuming. Meeting a minister is very difficult: make a written application to meet their special assistant or chief director instead. Ministries are regularly being asked to account for missing funds. In 2008, the government embarked on a big cost-cutting exercise throughout the ministries.

BUSINESS DRESS

The importance Ghanaians attach to
looking smart has already been
discussed. In a business
environment, this is of the utmost
importance. Men in top positions
will wear immaculate suits, or at
the very minimum, shining shoes
and well ironed trousers and shirt.
Women will be in trouser suits or long
skirts and matching blouses. It's common
in banks, for example, for all the women to be
wearing a wax print cloth with the bank's logo.
Traditional dress can still be considered smart
business attire, so you can expect to see *batakari*
and *kente* in the boardroom, along with the suits
and ties. Ghanaians are far from impressed with
any foreign businessperson who fails to dress
appropriately.

WOMEN IN BUSINESS

Despite the Victorian gender values already
mentioned, women at high levels in business or
government are given as much respect as men in
equivalent positions. Foreign businesswomen will
always be viewed as businesspeople first and
women second.

chapter **nine**

COMMUNICATING

LANGUAGE

Ghana has over fifty different local languages or dialects, but the national language is English, and whether you're living in Ghana or simply visiting, you can get by very well without using any local language. On the whole, Ghanaians are intelligent, well-educated, and sociable people and almost everyone you meet, especially in a professional capacity, will speak very good English. The language of the workplace and of instruction in schools for children over seven is English. Many television and radio programs are broadcast in English and you will hear English-language music. Signboards, official forms, menus, newspapers, and schoolbooks are all written in English. When making a purchase, the amount is always quoted in English. You can attend English-language church services and other events. Because Ghana has several Francophone neighbors, French is also heard.

Different Ghanaians speak English to different degrees, and, with very few exceptions, Ghanaians always learn one or more local languages before learning English. These different mother tongues naturally express something inherent and idiosyncratic to Ghanaian culture, something which can be lost in translation. Yes, you can get by with English, but you may have to forsake establishing meaningful relations with whole swaths of people, including children, uneducated people, the elderly, some vendors, and families from poor or isolated communities. Strong regional or national English accents, including American, can be difficult for Ghanaians to understand. Foreigners can often become frustrated by language barriers affecting their daily or working lives, even to the extent of leaving their jobs and going home.

Thousands of tourists come to Ghana every year and enjoy a perfect vacation without speaking a word of any Ghanaian language; indeed, foreign business and tourism are at such high levels that it is entirely possible to spend almost all one's social time in predominantly expat circles. Curiously, some people seem to decide to do just that. Many foreign workers who have been working for some years in Ghana can't even say "How are you?" in a Ghanaian language. There is no practical need for you to learn a local language, but you will be missing out on a lot if you don't. Learning a local language shows people respect, and in Ghana even the most faltering attempts are warmly welcomed. There is no reason why anybody who is in Ghana for any length of time should not at least be able to say "Hello" and "Thank you." At worst, some people may consider it rude if you don't. Conversely, speaking some of the language can offer you remarkable benefits, and help you to integrate easily into the rich Ghanaian culture and gain a deeper understanding of it. You can learn how to haggle, ask for and understand directions, join in with the common practice of sending children to do things for you, and develop a repertoire of witty remarks for when people in the street shout at white people walking by. On certain occasions, it would be customary to use some vernacular, for example when visiting a chief, speaking at a funeral, or praying before a meal.

With some exceptions, when Ghanaians talk among themselves they tend to use their own language. So you could be sitting in a bar, bus, office, or under a tree drinking palm wine, without a clue what everybody's talking about. Wouldn't you like to join in a bit, share the jokes, ask a few questions? And when other people are obviously talking about you, understanding them can stop you from thinking the worst.

It is possible to gain great success with only a few key phrases. You can learn by heart basic phrases such as "My name is . . ."; "I am from . . ."; "My job is . . ."; "Yes, I am / No, I'm not married . . ."; because that's what everyone who meets you will ask you. Try to "manage" conversations so you only say what you can. And it's common even when speaking the vernacular for Ghanaians to use lots of English, so do the same and just pop in the few local words that you do know.

The most useful language to learn is Twi, spoken by well over half the population, and the main local language used in music and films. Twi is the main language in the southern half of the country, where most tourists spend their time. The other big ones are Ga, Ewe, and Hausa. Pidgin English is very widespread among the youth. Listening to Pidgin English, which is basically corrupted English words in an African sentence structure, can give you a good idea of the formation and structure of Ghanaian languages.

Nonverbal Language

Learning some hand gestures and nonverbal language can help you to communicate and ensure you don't insult someone unintentionally.

Holding out an arm with the palm down, then quickly closing the fingers, means "Come here." This can be preceded by a loud clap if the person is far away. "Hissing" is another common way of gaining someone's attention.

Stroking the left palm with the right index finger, or rubbing a thumb and index finger together, is the universal sign meaning "money."

Pointing at somebody with the thumb, or biting the thumb then flicking it toward the person, is the equivalent of raising the middle finger in the US or the "V" sign in the UK. It is most often seen between irate taxi drivers, and can be accompanied by the very rude "*Wo maame!*" ("Your mother!").

Holding a flat hand palm down, then quickly flipping it up, represents asking a question; this is usually used between drivers and potential passengers to mean "Where are you going?."

Other transport gestures include pointing in the air in the general direction of where you're going to see if the driver is going in the same direction, and an up-and-down movement of the whole right arm to flag down a vehicle. In Accra, pointing toward the floor and making small circles with the index finger means you are heading toward Nkrumah Circle, Accra's main transport hub. Listen for the drivers shouting "Circ! Circ! Circ!"

You will rarely need any sign to flag down an Accra taxi driver. You'll get dozens of them beeping their horns at you and stopping to pick you up when you're not even going anywhere. Flicking the back of the hand toward somebody (the opposite of "come") means, obviously, "Go away."

Sucking the teeth or repeatedly clicking the tongue is a sign of disapproval: a single click of the tongue can mean "Yes."

Touching your right thumb and fingertips to your lips means "Eat," and touching the nearside of your right fist to your lips means "Drink." With palms up, tapping the palm of the left and the back of the right hand together means "I beg you."

Ghanaians are very tactile and will encroach upon what some Westerners may view as their personal space. Hugging, hand-holding, and close proximity are common between friends and peers, but usually only between members of the same sex. Men will sometimes be seen being flirtatious with a woman, but very rarely vice versa. With chiefs, elders, and seniors at work, body language is much more formal and shows a great deal of deference.

COMMUNICATION SERVICES
Telephone

Ghana currently has around half a million landlines, mostly with Ghana Telecom (taken over in 2009 by Vodafone), and around four million mobile phone subscribers with MTN, Tigo, Zain, and Kasapa (meaning "good talking"). Visitors will find it easy to buy a SIM card to use in their own mobile phone, or to buy a phone in Ghana. Pay phones are common, as are girls sitting under big umbrellas on the roadside with phones to rent by the minute. A common and annoying practice in Ghana is "flashing," which is calling your phone and allowing it to ring only once—a message for you to call them back so they don't use their credit.

Mail

Overseas mail can take around a week, in and out. All towns have their post offices, but it's almost impossible to buy stamps elsewhere and find a nearby mailbox. Similarly, all collection of post requires a trip to your private post box at the post office. Postcards showing local scenes are for sale around most city post offices.

Packages may be opened on collection and a customs charge demanded, depending upon the value of the contents. It is not unknown for letters and packages (particularly around Christmas) to go missing. If your sender writes something like "Secondhand goods—no value" or "Ladies' sanitary products" on the package it can help to put off the unscrupulous postal worker. Sending cash through the post is ill-advised.

Internet

Internet cafés have sprung up in most towns, but the network can be slow. Laptops and PCs are for sale everywhere and landline or wireless connections are available. But the network can be slow.

The Media

Free speech is celebrated in Ghana, and this is reflected in the wide range of media, which is full of strong views, mainly on politics. Investigative reporting, scrutiny into perceived corruption, and giving a voice to public opinion are important roles of the media. Around eighty local or national radio stations are in existence. Peace FM, Happy FM, and Joy FM are just some of the names that reflect

Ghana's outlook on life. Three TV stations—GTV, Metro TV, and TV3—are in competition with a growing number of satellite channels. Any of the numerous newspaper stands will offer the reader a huge selection of broadsheet and tabloid papers, the most popular being the *Daily Graphic.* Any old newspaper used as toilet paper or to wrap food is known as "graphic."

CONCLUSION

Ghana has its share of paradoxes and annoyances, but it remains a wonderful place to live, work, or visit. Its attractions cater to the whole gamut of foreign interests, from tourists simply looking for sunshine, a five-star hotel, a golden beach, and cool beer, to those who prefer a more culturally enlightening village visit, historical tour, or ecotourism experience, and those who are looking to do business in a growing economy. Ghana is rapidly developing an excellent reputation among travelers who are looking for a genuine African experience without fear of crime, hassle, underdevelopment, or lack of facilities.

Despite its various problems, Ghana has seen great progress since becoming the first black African country to gain independence more than fifty years ago. It is a beacon of democracy and stability on the continent. This development is continuing apace, and all the right wheels are in motion in order for it to achieve its goal of becoming a middle-income country with decent education, good health, and jobs for all.

We have seen that it is the Ghanaians themselves who are responsible for making Ghana the gem that it is. They have, with reason, been described as the friendliest people in the world. They are also a proud and patriotic people who want to present the best possible picture of their country to visitors. Ghana has not escaped globalization, or the Westernization of its many citizens living abroad, but traditional cultural values remain a strong influence in the daily lives of Ghanaians, especially where human relations and respect for others are concerned.

Getting beyond the "tourist bubble," or going the extra mile to get to know the people and their culture, is the best way to gain from your visit to the country and appreciate its qualities. Learning at least a little of a local language will go a very long way to achieving this. Visitors are warmly welcomed and well catered to, and if they demonstrate a little patience and understanding there will be few barriers and frustrations in the way of their enjoyment. Only a tiny minority go away with anything negative to say about the country or its people. In the words of a Ghanaian who was asked to describe his own country: "Ghana is cool. And hot."

Further Reading

Armah, Ayi Kwei. *The Beautiful Ones Are Not Yet Born*. London: Heinemann, 1988.

Briggs, Phillip. *Ghana*. London: Bradt Travel Guides, 2007.

Buah, F.A. *A History of Ghana*. London: Macmillan, 1980.

Gyekye, Kwame. *African Cultural Values*. Accra: Sankofa, 1996.

Ham, Anthony, et al. *Lonely Planet West Africa*. London/Oakland/Melbourne/Paris: Lonely Planet, 2006.

Kuada, John, and Yao Chachah. *Ghana: Understanding the People and Their Culture*. Accra: Woeli, 1999.

No More Worries: The Indispensable Insiders' Guide to Accra. Accra: North American Women's Association, 1997.

Utley, Ian. *M'adamfo! The Essential Guide for all Obronis in Ghana*. Accra: SEDCO, 2008.

Ward, W.E.F. *My Africa*. Accra: Ghana Universities Press, 1991.

CULTURAL TOUR WEB SITES

www.discoveringghanacompany.org
www.culturalcollaborative.org
www.gapyearghana.org
www.womeninprogress.org
www.primetoursghana.org

Copyright © 2009 Kuperard
Revised 2010; fifth printing 2013

All rights reserved. No part of this publication may be reprinted or reproduced, stored in a retrieval system, or transmitted in any form or by any means without prior permission in writing from the publishers.

Culture Smart!® is a registered trademark of Bravo Ltd.

Index

Acknowledgments

To Ben and Ruby Otoo and my three goddaughters, Baaba, Nana Adwoa,
and Naa. Thank you for your friendship, kindness, and hospitality.

This book is dedicated to my late father, John Neville Utley (1937–2008):
my own "walking dictionary."